# CHILDREN, TELEVISION, AND SEX-ROLE STEREOTYPING

## Frederick Williams, Robert LaRose, and Frederica Frost

PRAEGER

PRAEGER SPECIAL STUDIES • PRAEGER SCIENTIFIC

**Library of Congress Cataloging in Publication Data**

Williams, Frederick, 1933-
   Children, television, and sex-role stereotyping.

   Bibliography: p.
   Includes indexes.
   1. Television and children.  2. Sex role.
3. Stereotype (Psychology)  I. La Rose, Robert,
joint author.  II. Frost, Frederica, joint author.
III. Title.
HQ784.T4W488     791.45'01'3     80-27500
ISBN 0-03-058303-9

*This book is based partly upon reports developed
under a subcontract from National Institute of Education,
Contract No. 400-76-0096. The views expressed do not
necessarily reflect those of the National Institute of
Education nor any agency of the U.S. Government.*

Published in 1981 by Praeger Publishers
CBS Educational and Professional Publishing
A Division of CBS, Inc.
521 Fifth Avenue, New York, New York 10175 U.S.A.

# FOREWORD

If just a single picture is worth anything close to the prover-
bial thousand words, then the amount of information contained in a
half-hour television program staggers the imagination. When that
figure is multiplied to take into account the four hours of television
the average child watches each day, the sheer magnitude of information children obtain from this medium over the course of a year is
mind boggling. It is no wonder, then, that social scientists have
been interested in investigating what the content of this information
is, who ought to control it, and most important, what its impact is
upon the developing child.

Over the past decade both the public and the scientific com-
munities have actively debated these issues. A considerable number of studies have been conducted documenting the nature of the
content of children's programs and their commercial messages.
Initially, there was primary concern over the amount of aggression
depicted and its possible effects upon children's behavior. This
concern continues, but more recently, interest has centered on the
ways in which children learn from television about social roles.

Pervasive stereotyping characterizes the ways in which sex
roles are portrayed on television. The situation has been recently
summarized by Feshbach, Dillman, and Jordan: "In sum, the programs which are specifically designed for children do not present
appropriate models from which young girls can learn that they are
worthwhile, capable and appreciated by society." This rather
sweeping statement is based upon a review of the evidence, which
consistently shows the same insidious pattern: Women are serious-
ly underrepresented on television; they are portrayed in very limited occupational roles (if at all); and they are shown as typically
deriving their identity from relationships with others.

Recent studies suggest that such statistics are merely the tip
of an iceberg. Henderson, Greenberg, and Atkin (1980), for example, maintain that when actual behavior patterns are examined in
depth, sex-role stereotypes are revealed as not merely evident in
frequencies but as "woven deeply into the television programming
fabric." According to the analyses of these latter investigators,
men give orders more frequently than women on television (even
after the initial disproportion in frequency of gender presentation is
allowed for), their orders are obeyed more often, and they very
rarely ask anyone for emotional support, even when it is needed.

v

Interestingly, although the major focus of investigators in this area has been upon the negative effects on girls, it could certainly be argued on the basis of results such as these that the effects must be equally devastating for boys. The limitations placed upon what is allowable as "appropriate" masculine behavior may well have implications for why males develop more stress-related diseases.

It should be noted that while there is wide agreement regarding the type of sex-role stereotyping children are exposed to, there is less agreement about its specific effects. There are a number of problems inherent in demonstrating specificity from a tendency that seems so pervasive. The case can be made, for example, that children are exposed to stereotyping in many areas—in the books they read, in their school environment, in their parents' socialization practices, and in their friends' beliefs. How much, then, can actually be attributed to television?

Researchers have attempted to provide answers to this question by a number of means. One method has relied upon correlational evidence. It has been found that children who watch a large amount of television (Freueh and McGhee, 1975) tend to accept more stereotypes than those who watch with less frequency. In a similar vein, recent work conducted in our own laboratory (Katz, 1980) suggests that the traditional content of children's television preferences is a more reliable predictor of their future sex-role expectations than the socialization practices of their parents. A second technique has involved assessing the effects of viewing nontraditional sex-role content. Several positive findings suggest that even small-scale efforts can make a difference. Commercials depicting women in nontraditional roles, for example, elicit less traditional beliefs about women after the manipulation (for example, Atkins and Miller, 1975; Pingree, 1978).

The research described in this book is of particular importance because it was integrally related to the production and evaluation of Freestyle, a series specifically designed to teach children that sex roles can indeed be flexible. Amidst the relatively limited modeling possibilities presently available on children's television, this program represents a welcome change.

The studies described in this volume have several advantages over earlier work aimed at changing children's attitudes toward sex roles. First, the investigators had direct and ready access to the televised materials. Second, they were able to develop more sustained intervention strategies than others have used.

The results of these studies are closer to life than to television in that they are not simple and clear-cut. The findings suggest that there are sex-related differences in receptivity to nontraditional sex-role messages. Boys are not only less receptive but may occasionally show "boomerang" effects. The authors also raise important questions based on their findings about the over-simplistic conceptual models used by many investigators in this area. Both this research and other recent work show that grade-school children have highly differentiated cognitive structures about sex roles. This finding has several implications. On a pragmatic level, it suggests that future modification efforts may need to be aimed at younger groups. From a social science viewpoint, it suggests that change measures may require greater dimensionality and that theoretical views may require increased complexity.

Life portrayed on television is always simpler than life in the laboratory. The questions raised here are of great importance for future researchers, however, and it is gratifying to see such a significant start being made in the right direction.

Phyllis A. Katz, Ph.D.

# ACKNOWLEDGMENTS

Much credit, we feel, must be given to the National Institute of Education for their insistence on a major research component in the Television Career Awareness Project and for the necessary funds to sponsor it. Since most of the compilation of this volume came after the duration of the project, we must also acknowledge the Annenberg School of Communications at the University of Southern California for encouraging completion of a broadly distributed report of our research.

Certain scholars have had influential effects upon our work. These include the early suggestions of Aletha Huston-Stein, our on-going collaboration with Esther Diamond and Jerome Johnson, and the follow-up exchanges with Janet Taylor Spence and Phyllis Katz. We want to be certain, however, to acknowledge them for their influence on us and not their endorsement of what follows.

We would like to extend a warm note of gratitude to television producer Norton Wright whose practical insights sometimes tested our theories more rapidly than if we had been dealing with pins and balloons. Most important was that we usually came back with something better.

Staff members Harvey Eastman, Claudia Wright, and Renate Faber were invaluable for their individual contributions. Consultant Pat Seeley kept us in touch with the teacher and classroom environments.

But beyond all of the above good people, we would like to dedicate this volume to those hundreds of fourth-, fifth-, and sixth-grade children who participated so wholeheartedly in our research. The future is truly theirs.

# CONTENTS

xi

LIST OF TABLES

## LIST OF FIGURES

# 1

# A RADICAL PROPOSAL

In 1975 the Television Career Awareness Project (TV CAP) was formed with the goal of using television and associated materials to combat sex-role stereotyping in 9- to 12-year-old children. The project eventually led to the development of the public television series "Freestyle," which has now been established as highly successful in its positive influences on children.* In the mid-1970s it was a controversial proposition that television, which so typically abounds in stereotypes, might be used to promote more balanced social attitudes. Moreover, the period also marked the beginning of a veritable revolution in the conceptualization and measurement of sex-role biases in children.

This book reports our research into these challenging yet intriguing areas—research that although useful in the formation of "Freestyle" transcends it to be of interest to others concerned with the general intersection of children, television, and sex-role stereotyping.

## ON STEREOTYPING AND STEREOTYPES

Particularly with the rise of the women's movement in the 1970s, considerable practical and theoretical interest has emerged in the acquisition of sex roles by children. Such interest has been marked by an attempt to analyze boy-girl differences that are not

---

*The effects of "Freestyle" have been well documented (Johnston & Ettema, in preparation; Johnston, Ettema, & Davidson, 1980).

1

directly attributable to biological contrast but are more a heritage of the social environment of growing up. Thus, it is blue for boys, pink for girls, dolls or toy trucks, sewing versus model building, and eventually in adulthood being a waitress, nurse, or secretary in contrast to being a laborer, doctor, or businessman.

A term with particularly pejorative connotations in this area is sex-role stereotyping. In its usual application, this term has referred to relatively fixed beliefs, opinions, or attitudes that individuals hold about typical characteristics of boys and girls or men and women. These may relate to personality (boys are tough and insensitive, girls are weak and sensitive), occupations (women are nurses, men are engineers), or activity interests (girls like to play house, boys like to play cops and robbers), to name a few. The problem with such stereotypes, most have contended, is that they impose unnecessary differentiations between men and women; they restrict opportunities for individual growth; they bias our ability to see males and females as individuals.

A number of studies (Busby, 1974; Long & Simon, 1971; Seggar & Wheeler, 1973; U.S. Civil Rights Commission, 1977) by 1977 had claimed a substantial bias in men outnumbering women in television portrayals, occupying higher status positions, and exhibiting a greater range of positive personality characteristics. It was a challenge that a major project envisaged to combat sex-role stereotyping would use television as its chief medium. Such circumstances eventually gave birth to the TV CAP, which produced "Freestyle," a television series designed to combat sex-role stereotyping in 9- to 12-year-old children in the United States. Complementing the series were printed materials for children, teachers, and parents. The series first aired on public broadcasting stations in the fall and winter of 1978/79.


APPROACH

The present studies were conducted as a part of formative research underlying the development of "Freestyle." Formative research, particularly well known from the "Sesame Street" example, involves a close liaison between researchers and the creative personnel in the production process. Because of the pressure of production schedules, such research is often more practical than theoretical and more ad hoc and hurried than is the typical development of social scientific research. But because "Freestyle" was breaking new ground in educational and public television, there was both a need and a budget provision for a theoretical inquiry into sex-role stereotyping in children.

This book is a summary of such studies, including those centered upon a fundamental question, What are useful conceptualizations of sex-role stereotyping in children? Because we were dealing with a phenomenon thought by many to be affected in part by the television medium—let alone that the television medium was also to be an intervention strategy—research was also shaped by a constituent question, How might television experiences affect sex-role stereotyping?

In the communications field, research into this general area has mainly comprised the content analytic studies of sex roles as portrayed on television. These have been of little theoretical value to us, since they generally beg the question of which content has a detailed effect upon the viewer. Most important, these studies have not touched upon a fundamental conceptualization of how children acquire social beliefs, attitudes, and, eventually, behavioral strategies from television. In the present research, we hope to have taken a step in this direction.

Chapters 2 and 3 summarize the prior and ongoing literature that we have found influential to our thinking.

Chapters 4 through 7 report our original research in the replication of selected measures of sex-role stereotyping in children.

Chapter 8 describes our study of relations between sex-role biases of children and their reactions to counterstereotypic television characters.

Chapters 9 through 11 describe the consequences of our theoretical shift away from a global concept of sex-role stereotyping in children and the contribution of Martin Fishbein's "expectancy value" theory to this area.

Chapters 12 and 13 are further inquiries into expectancy value theory but now include television media variables in the model.

Finally, Chapter 14 outlines our tentative theory of at least one process by which television may affect a child's attitudes and behaviors and, eventually, social strategies.

# 2

## STEREOTYPING AND PSYCHOLOGICAL SEX

Although the literature on sex roles is copious, most of the research into stereotyping per se is relatively recent, and only currently (late 1970s, early 1980s) is it truly converging along sound theoretical lines. As mentioned in Chapter 1, we found ourselves in the beginnings of a revolution in thinking, particularly on the stereotype issue and its measurement. In this chapter, we review work that has been useful to us—more specifically, useful because it provided either background or insights into strategies for changing stereotypes. Some of the literature in this chapter was not yet available to us as we began our initial research. Nevertheless, our results eventually showed remarkable consistency with what has evolved, despite differences in subject populations and the exact concept domains examined.

We recognized at the start the many problems in researching children's sex-role biases, among these the imposition of adult stereotypes upon the measures employed, the abstract nature of the traits involved, the apparent sex bias of the concepts (for example, boys may be reticent to admit they feel anxiety [Mischel, 1970]), and even contamination due to the sex of the experimenter (Mischel, 1970; Williams, Bennett, & Best, 1975). Despite the difficulties, we desired to replicate aspects of some of these earlier studies, seeking not only comparability regarding sex differentiation but regarding ethnic and age breakdowns as well. The current chapter presents a review of the sex-role literature relevant to our project, including those later studies with implications for our own results.

## SEX-ROLE DEVELOPMENT

In confronting possible strategies for changing children's attitudes and beliefs, important factors appeared to be the evolution of the child's conception of sex role and the appearance of sex-appropriate behavior. While a detailed explication of the various facets of this subject represents an undertaking beyond the scope of this volume, we nevertheless present a brief summary of existing theories, the purpose being to provide a basis upon which to build a theoretical foundation. In view of conflicting definitions in the literature, we shall broadly define sex-role development as the acquisition of knowledge regarding sex-appropriate behaviors and attributes (the sex-role standard [Kagan, 1964]) and their integration into the individual's self-concept in the forms of beliefs, attitudes, and behaviors.

Three general modes of thought have reflected the diverse influences in the development of sex roles: identification, as represented by Freudian theory; environmental, commonly labeled social learning theory (Mischel, 1970); and cognitive theory (Kohlberg, 1966). Freudian thought involves the early identification of both male and female child with the mother, the male later shifting to the father. Social learning theory and cognitive theory both involve rewards and reinforcement in sex-role development, but while social learning theorists suggest that rewards for sex-appropriate behavior lead to gender identity, Kohlberg posits that gender identity comes first, followed by sex-appropriate behavior, which is then rewarding and satisfying. Succinctly expressed, identification and social learning theory assume a rather passive individual under environmental press, while the Kohlberg view involves an interaction between the child and his or her surroundings (Katz, 1979). According to Kohlberg (1966), neither biological givens nor social mores precede sex-role development; rather, it is due to the "child's cognitive organization of his social world along sex-role dimensions" (p. 82), this patterning dependent at various stages in development upon the individual's level of cognitive maturity.

Similar to the measurement of masculinity and femininity, traditional conceptions of sex-role development are undergoing a period of criticism and change. For example, Maccoby and Jacklin (1974) conclude that only aggression among sex-related attributes may be biologically based, refuting the concept of innate differences between the sexes in a wide variety of behaviors and characteristics.

The primary criticism of Kohlberg's cognitive theory appears to be the late age (approximately five years) at which sexual constancy appears, defined as the realization that a person's sex is a permanent characteristic. Such an understanding Kohlberg considers integral to a stable sex identity, although Maccoby and Jacklin (1974) do not believe that gender constancy is necessary for the child to begin the adoption of sex-appropriate behavior. Further, Kohlberg's position directly contradicts evidence that changing the assigned sex of children of ambiguous gender after the age of two can be problematic for the individual's psychological adjustment (Katz, 1979; Constantinople, 1979), indicative of some degree of very early stability in gender identity.

Social learning has not gone unscathed in facing the brunt of criticism. Modeling forms a basis of this position, yet based on a comprehensive literature review, Maccoby and Jacklin (1974) suggest that modeling plays a relatively minor part in sex-role development, applicable only within a very narrow range of behaviors, such as dresses for girls, but inadequate as an explanation for broader classes of behavior. For example, they cite the lack of similarity between children and the parents after whom they purportedly model (a view shared by Katz, 1979), and the lack of evidence that same-sex models are more available in American society for modeling purposes.

A final problem with all the above views, noted by Katz (1979), is the bias due to the sex of the theorist, the majority of whom are male. In general, theories center around the male with the female as a kind of adjunct and viewed primarily from her desire to be masculine. Katz proposes an alternate model based upon the assumption that sex-role development begins in infancy and continues as a life-long process. Three broad, overlapping developmental levels include the following: (1) learning the appropriate behavior for the male and female child, (2) acquisition of concepts regarding what is appropriate as a potential female or male adult, and (3) exhibiting behavior appropriate to the female or male adult over the life span. Sub-stages are specified within each of these general areas, and the focus is primarily on the female. Katz emphasizes that the tasks at each level may differ for members of each sex and that each stage may carry with it a different set of social influences.

Constantinople (1979) has proposed a sex-as-rules model in an attempt to compensate for inadequacies in earlier theories. Drawing from both social learning and cognitive tenets, she proposes that the young child's early capacities to screen sex-role information are probably derived from an interaction among innate abilities to categorize, generalize, and discriminate sex-related information contained in the environment. Reinforcement serves the purpose of increasing the salience of particular sex-related behaviors and marking them with either positive or negative affect. Constantinople draws on the young child's need for cognitive structure and appears to accept Kohlberg's theorizing as it applies to a stable gender identification at about age 5. In the initial stages of the child's development, she posits that words are used as labeling devices for sex-related characteristics and later supplemented by other environmental cues such as hairstyles and clothing.

## RELATIONSHIP OF THE SEX-ROLE STANDARD TO SEX-ROLE STEREOTYPING

The study of stereotypes dates to Walter Lippmann's first use of the term (Lippmann, 1922), with subsequent research generally aimed at attitudes toward racial groups. Sex-role stereotyping represents a relatively newer area of research with earlier studies concentrating on roles appropriate to females and males and the subsequent attribution of these characteristics prescribed culturally to each sex and across ethnic boundaries. While definitions of stereotype abound, we begin here with the one by Mackie (1973), as it resulted from an extensive literature review. Stereotypes were defined as "those folk beliefs about the attributes characterizing a social category on which there is substantial agreement" (p. 435). Thus, females are supposed to be gentle, dependent, and social, while males are expected to show strength, interest in science and math, and independence, among other characteristics and behaviors that may be either socially positive or negative.

Recall that the sex-role standard comprises the behaviors and characteristics culturally assigned to one sex or the other; the standard's components may be assumed to be primarily positive characteristics. However, the manner in which we used the term stereotype in the "Freestyle" project reaches beyond simple beliefs regarding a social category. Our mandate decreed that we combat sex-role stereotypes. The implication here is that something negative exists that requires elimination, and this is reflected in our working definition of sex-role stereotype—specifically, beliefs about a biological category that tend to be exaggerated and that serve as a mechanism through which equal opportunity to resources is denied to its members. As a rather obvious example, let us take the female-stereotyped attribute "emotional," a characteristic that carries with it the implication of a lack of logical thinking ability and the belief that females lose their composure in tight situations, which then becomes a reason for keeping them in full, low-paying jobs that do not require quick, rational decision making.

In the sex-role standard, the child is presented a highly attractive constellation of characteristics, which, in most cases, is enthusiastically adopted. It is only as the individual grows older that the less desirable aspects of the mandate may become evident. Enter the sex-role stereotype. The realization of the undesirable components of their standard becomes evident much earlier to girls than to boys, who are less likely to perceive that society has limited their choices in what they might become. The clear message girls receive—that theirs is the less desirable sex—renders the sex-role standard, as well as stereotyping, a much more negative experience for them than for their male peers (Flerx, Fidler, & Rogers, 1976; Kohlberg, 1966).

Furthermore, early theorists assumed that adoption of the attributes composing the appropriate standard represents a highly desirable and necessary phase in the individual's development (Kagan, 1964; Kohlberg, 1966; Mussen, 1969). Evidence is beginning to accrue, however, to suggest that the unequivocal adoption of the standard appropriate for one's own sex, at least in a total sense, may not be desirable (Bem & Lenney, 1976; Spence & Helmreich, 1978).

## PSYCHOLOGICAL SEX

In the older literature on sex-role development, the case in which an individual does not adopt the sex role congruent with his or her biological sex or, less drastically, adopts characteristics from standards of both sexes is viewed as abnormal, or deviant at the very least. Masculinity and femininity are generally conceived as mutually exclusive categories, not only biologically but in certain aspects of psychological functioning as well. Those adopting a sex-role identity opposite from their own biological sex, either as a result of parenting or improper biological classification (in a Freudian sense, for example), may experience personality difficulties and emotional problems (Brown, 1957). The case of adopting characteristics of both sex-role standards, however, is not explicitly treated. The concept that views the degree to which an individual has adopted feminine and masculine characteristics as separate entities is a relatively new one in psychology and enables the placement of a person on separate scales of femininity and masculinity. This is what we have termed the individual's psychological sex, which differs from sex-role identity in its connotation of greater freedom of attribute adoption and behavior for the individual. Categorically knowing a person's psychological sex should therefore provide considerably more information regarding a rather broad constellation of personality characteristics than knowing biological sex alone.

We discuss the measurement implications of psychological sex in a later section, but for now let us say that it allows various combinations of individuals on these two dimensions, masculinity and femininity. For example, those who describe themselves in terms of a high number of masculine characteristics and a low number of feminine ones may be labeled masculine. Conversely, those high in feminine characteristics and low in masculine ones are feminine. What of those high in both? One term for these individuals is androgynous (Bem, 1974)—possessing a high number of socially positive attributes characteristic of each sex. "Undifferentiated" people, on the other hand, are low in both feminine and masculine attributes (Spence, Helmreich, & Stapp, 1974). According to Bem (1974; Bem & Lenney, 1976; Bem, Martyna, & Watson, 1976), androgynous people should be more flexible, adaptable, and psychologically healthier than sex-typed individuals.

This new conceptualization is particularly seductive if, as with "Freestyle," it is from the viewpoint of a change agent. Indeed, if traditional thinking regarding masculinity and femininity is erroneous, then the adoption of masculine attributes by girls no longer precludes their retaining the nucleus of their feminine identity. The reverse would be true for males. This has tremendous implications for social change, primarily in that it dramatically reduces the radical nature of the task of combating the effects of sex-role stereotypes. Rather than eradicating the individual's entire self-concept and replacing it with another representing the opposite pole of a continuum, the task becomes one of supplementing personality attributes with characteristics that result in a psychologically healthier individual.

However, quite a distance separates the elimination of sex-role stereotypes from changes in self-concept in the area of psychological sex. Ratings of others (most boys, most girls, ideal woman, ideal man), which may be assumed to measure stereotypes (at least in the absence of information other than biological sex), do not necessarily correspond to ratings of self (Guttentag & Bray, 1976; Spence & Helmreich, 1978). This presents difficulties in planning change—that is, does one attack the stereotype of the self-concept directly? The answer is not yet entirely clear, and questions have arisen regarding the validity of the older instruments as well as the new.

Other difficulties remain regarding the concept of psychological sex, both on measurement and theoretical grounds, and the relationship of psychological sex to behavior is also under scrutiny. However, before the denouement, we trace the evolution of the measurement of masculinity and femininity from the bipolar to the unidemensional and, finally, to the current state of the art.

## MEASUREMENT OF SEX-ROLE STEREOTYPES
## AND PSYCHOLOGICAL SEX

Studies in the measurement of sex-role stereotypes and psychological sex can be divided into two distinct categories: those employing the "old" operationalization of a bipolar masculinity-femininity and those operating under a dualistic approach similar to Constantinople's (1973) reconceptualization. Although at first glance these earlier instruments may appear outdated, current thinking in the area appears to suggest that the concepts that form their basis are not entirely erroneous.

Two general characteristics differentiate the old instruments from the new. The first, a pervasive component of these older instruments, is the assumption of bipolarity in the concept "male-female," precluding the possibility of an individual's possessing characteristics of both sexes. Hence, a high degree of femininity automatically signifies a low degree of masculinity. The second discriminating factor is that many older measures include items from several domains. This is particularly true of psychological scales in which personal attributes are mixed with behaviors.

The older-generation tests may be classified into three subgroups: those assessing aspects of masculinity and femininity in the areas of preference, memory, and knowledge; occupational beliefs; and psychological attributes. We review selected instruments in each of these areas, particularly from the perspective of research in children and our own desire to measure their stereotyped beliefs and psychological sex.

The majority of instruments were designed to measure sex-role preferences, or the degree to which a child responds sex-appropriately. The researcher assumes, for example, that the child who chooses female-typed toys has a female sex-role preference, and similarly for male-typed toys. The object preference tests require only that the subject point to an object, as in choosing a doll or toy truck. Language requirements remain minimal, and for that reason these methods are ideal for use with young children.

Probably the best known of these tests is the It Scale for Children (Brown, 1957) in which the child designates what "It" would like to play with or what "It" would like to be from a variety of sex-typed items. "It" is a stick figure with ambiguous gender for whom the child is asked to make choices regarding a variety of objects and activities. On a sample of 5- to 11-year-old children, Brown (1957) found a large proportion of girls who preferred the male role; subsequent research has replicated this effect, which may be due, it has been suggested, to the more masculine than feminine appearance of "It" (Kohlberg, 1966) or to the generic use of male responses in girls (McCandless, 1967, cited in Ward, 1969). For a review of further studies with a revised "It," see Fling and Manosevitz (1972).

Vener and Snyder (1966) used sex-typed objects ("artifacts") to assess $2\frac{1}{2}$- to 22-year-old children's sex-role preferences. Children were first asked to whom a particular object belonged ("Mommy" or "Daddy"), then which five the subject most wanted for himself or herself. Vener and Snyder found that the youngest children of $2\frac{1}{2}$ years made 74.7 percent "correct" responses with the proportion of right choices increasing with age. Girls and boys did not differ in the number of correct answers, but girls showed a higher preference for the same sex-typed items in comparison with boys until approximately the age of 5 years.

Nadelman (1974) measured knowledge of memory and preference for sex-typed items in 5- to 9-year-old subjects. Children were assessed in three areas, as follows: (1) recall of pictures of sex-typed items after seeing them presented and named by the experimenter, (2) matching pictures of sex-typed items to a drawing of "Susie" or "Tommy," according to whom the items belong or went best with, and (3) choice of a number of the best-liked items. Results indicated that subjects recalled more of their same-sex items and more with increasing age. Regarding the knowledge test (matching items with Susie or Tommy), middle-class and older children scored higher. Preference scores showed that boys limited their choices to same-sex items more than girls.

Flerx et al. (1976) used a doll technique to assess a wide variety of sex-role attitudes in 3-, 4-, and 5-year-old children. Subjects were shown girl and boy dolls, or mother and father dolls, and were allowed to choose both if desired. Through these, attitudes were examined in a variety of sex-stereotyped areas. Analysis indicated that the 4- and 5-year-old children gave more stereotypic responses than the 3-year-olds and that the males were more stereotypic in one of the six areas assessed.

DeLucia's Toy Preference Test (DeLucia, 1963) for kindergarten through fourth-grade children consisted of paired pictures of sex-typed children's toys. These were accompanied by a small picture of a girl if the subject was female or a picture of a boy if the subject was male. A sum of the correct number of responses represented each child's score. If a pair presented consisted of two masculine toys, boys were expected to choose the one with the higher masculine rating, while girls were expected to choose the least masculine of the two. Boys made more correct choices than girls.

Within this class of instruments, one factor generally stands out: a "correct" score is usually one congruent with the sex-role standard. The child is "wrong" if she or he prefers cross-sex toys even though same-sex toys may also be liked. Similarly, only household items can correctly belong to Mommy; if a child's mother has a toolbox for household repairs and the child responds accordingly, the child and the mother are "wrong." This apparent rigidity of the sex-role standard is partly a reflection of the bipolar conception of masculinity-femininity; embracing one precludes the other.

Preference tests contain other difficulties, both psychometric and theoretical. For example, it is doubtful that sex-role identity or preference can be accurately assessed by asking a child which toy he or she would like to play with. Too many factors confound the results, such as the effects of novelty upon the child (toys not seen before may be more attractive), experimenter effects, and confounding caused by other toys from which the child can choose (differences in overall desirability, for example, as a new truck versus an old doll). In addition to these problems of reliability, questions regarding validity also emerge. It now appears evident that sex-role development is a highly complex process resulting in the multidimensional factors of psychological sex. Sears, Rau, and Alpert (1965) point this out clearly in their study of nursery school children. They employed several different measures of sex-role development but found, in general, low correlations among them and concluded that the areas of sex typing are not yet well integrated by the time the child reaches nursery school age. The implication here is, of course, that at some time the various facets of sex roles do become integrated; however, there still exists little evidence to suggest that measures of sex typing will yield integration at any age level.

Further, the relationship of behavior to measures of psychological sex is not necessarily correspondent but rather results from situational, social, and personal factors. Attempting to measure sex-role development with simple toy preference or knowledge measures in light of this consideration alone appears highly questionable.

Activity interests have also been the research focus in assessing sex-role preferences, one with a theoretical base in Kagan's (1964) emphasis on cultural games as integral to the development of sex-role identification. In one study, Rosenberg and Sutton-Smith (1959) examined differences in liking for 67 activities that differentiated between the preferences of girls and boys. Each item was assigned a value indicative of its power to discriminate by sex (for example, a "3" for activities differentiating at a $p$ level of greater than .01). Scores for each student were then summed and means calculated. Rosenberg and Sutton-Smith found a very small percentage of females falling above the mean for males on the masculine scale, and very few males above the mean on the female scale. They replicated these findings on two subsequent samples and concluded that the scales were of practical and theoretical value in examining sex-role identification in children.

In a later study, Fagot and Littman (1975) developed masculinity-femininity activity scores to assess the stability of interest
patterns over time. They used Tyler's test, which contains forced-
choice activity items (". . . tell me which one you like better").
Older children were individually questioned; the activities of preschool children were coded during playtimes. Masculinity and femininity scores were calculated, one set for the preschool subjects
and one for those in elementary school. Girls' and boys' scores differed significantly in the expected directions. Congruent with the
results of Rosenberg and Sutton-Smith (1959), no age trends in
scores reached significance. Also congruent with earlier results,
girls gave evidence of a wider variety of interests than boys (Rosenberg & Sutton-Smith, 1960). Fagot and Littman argue, however,
that assessing girls' activity interests may not measure femininity
in this area at all—that rather than interests per se, the underlying
factor may be the manner in which a girl orients herself toward those
around her. This is supported in their data by the large number of
responses given by girls that related to helping adults and also explains the greater variability of girls' interests in comparison with
boys' (Rosenberg & Sutton-Smith, 1959, 1960, 1964; Nadelman, 1974;
see also Stein, Pohly, & Mueller, 1971).

In assessing activities, both sets of researchers above—Rosenberg and Sutton-Smith and Fagot and Littman—deviated from the traditional masculine-feminine bipolarity and developed scales that allowed the subject to express an interest in both areas. Rather than
a deliberate innovation with implications for the entire realm of sex-
role research, however, this practice appears to have been specific
only to the measurement of activity preferences.

Assessment of sex-role stereotypes through beliefs about occupations is generally conducted for the purpose of examining aspects
of job discrimination and bias against females. Most studies of occupational stereotypes do not attempt to build masculinity-femininity
scales as such. Rather, they seek to classify occupations into categories of feminine, masculine, or neutral—both a priori and as a result of subject ratings—and then to assess the stereotypic aspects of
classification. Two primary methods exist to measure a person's
sex-role stereotyping of occupations. The first and simplest (obviously for children) is to ask about vocational preference ("What do
you want to do when you grow up?"). The second is to ask the subject to rate occupations on some kind of scale that usually connotes
the ability of men, women, or both to perform the job in question.

Studies of sex stereotyping of occupational preference have examined several aspects of the area, beyond the general finding that
children's responses are highly sex stereotyped (Beuf, 1974; Boynton,
1936; E. Clark, 1967). E. Clark (1967) noted a greater variety in

boys' responses than girls'. Socioeconomic status has been found
to be a factor confounding comparisons by sex (Boynton, 1936; E.
Clark, 1967), as has ethnic group membership (Leifer & Lesser,
1976). In general, findings are represented in the conclusion given
by Douvan and Adelson (1966) that most girls' choices of occupation
fall into the four traditional female categories of glamor-fashion,
white-collar traditional, personal aide, and social aide. Boys' responses in general constitute higher-status, higher-paying pursuits
(Barnett, 1975; Boynton, 1936; E. Clark, 1967). Even though children may report that women can be doctors, very few girls actually
choose this occupation (Schlossberg & Goodman, 1972).

Ratings by subjects regarding the ability of either sex to perform a particular job were used by Iglitzin (1972) to explore sex-role
stereotyping of occupations. Fifth-grade children were asked whether
"men," "women," or "both men and women" should perform particular jobs. Findings indicated that both boys and girls stereotyped job
categories but that girls were more willing to cross traditional lines.
Schlossberg and Goodman (1972) in a slight variation of the same
method showed pictures of work settings to elementary school children and asked them, for example, "This is where a person works
who fixes televisions and radios. Could a man work here? Could a
woman work here?" Question order and work sequence were ran-
domized. Schlossberg and Goodman found, much as Iglitzin did, a
high degree of "traditional" answers by the children; perceptions of
what women could do were much more limited than similar perceptions of males.

Garrett, Ein, and Tremaine (1977) expanded the measurement
instrument to yield a five-step scale that allowed respondents a
middle or "neutral" category to include both men and women. They
accompanied the scales with pictures in studying first-, third-, and
fifth-grade children. The child was asked about the ability of men
and women to perform each occupation. Results in general corroborated earlier studies in that children stereotyped occupations with
no differences between girls and boys on female-stereotyped occupations.

Psychological scales to measure sex stereotypes or psychological sex constitute the preponderance of early work in the field.
They also provided the source for the concept of psychological sex
in multidimensional space.

Bipolar scales of personality attributes with opposite traits at
each pole are predicated on the assumption that a high degree of
femininity corresponds to a low degree of masculinity and vice versa;
measurement on these scales does not allow a high score on both
concepts. The earliest studies using such measurement are represented by instruments such as the Terman-Miles M-F Test (Terman

& Miles, 1936), the Masculinity-Femininity scale on the Minnesota Multiphasic Psychological Inventory (Hathaway & McKinley, 1951), the California Psychological Inventory Fe Scale (Gough, 1952), and Guilford's Masculinity Scale (Guilford & Guilford, 1936).

## DUALISM: A NEW CONCEPTUALIZATION OF MASCULINITY AND FEMININITY

The lack of consistent definitions of masculinity and femininity in the older scales has been noted by Constantinople (1973). She also points out the correspondent lack of a basis upon which instruments could be developed and validated. These criticisms, and her call for a multidimensional conceptualization of masculinity and femininity, were followed by a flood of new instruments. Four of these are perhaps the best known: Bem Sex Role Inventory (BSRI) (Bem, 1974), Personal Attributes Questionnaire (PAQ) (Spence et al., 1974), PRF ANDRO Scale (Berzins, Welling, & Wetter, 1975), and Heilbrun's adaptation of the Adjective Check List (Gough & Heilbrun, 1965; Heilbrun, 1976). In addition, two instruments are available for use with children: the Sex Stereotype Measure (Williams et al., 1975) and the Semantic Differential Test (Guttentag & Bray, 1976). All the foregoing are predicated on an empirical basis similar to previous instruments, the ability of the instruments to differentiate males from females. Although not meant for use with children, we present a detailed examination of the BSRI and the PAQ, as they are central in the current quandary over the concept of androgyny, which in turn has been a factor in our own intervention effort.

In addition to embracing the premise that masculinity and femininity represent essentially independent dimensions, Bem's (1974) BSRI instrument has the following additional features. First, rather than item selection based on differences between women and men, items were chosen on the basis of sex-typed social desirability or traits differentially desirable for females and males. Second, three scores can be calculated for each respondent, a Masculinity score (M), a Femininity score (F), and an Androgyny score. And third, the scale provides a social desirability index through the use of neutral items.

Masculinity and femininity items were chosen from a pool of 200 that had been judged as socially desirable and sex typed in connotation. Subjects rated these for men and for women, as for example, "In American society, how desirable is it for a man to be truthful?" (Bem, 1974, p. 157). Items retained had ratings of significantly different desirability for a woman than for a man or vice versa: 20 feminine and 20 masculine items resulted from this process. Criteria for neutral items included lack of greater desirability for one sex over the other and agreement between female and male judges on trait desirability. On a 7-point scale, subjects were asked to describe themselves only. The scale, then, does not represent a test of sex stereotyping but rather one of psychological sex. Analysis of results indicated that raters agreed that the set of items for their own sex was highly desirable and those for the opposite sex less desirable. The M and F scales were essentially orthogonal. Correlations between M and F and social desirability were moderate, but so-called Androgyny scores with social desirability were near zero.

Bem originally suggested a balance method for scoring her instrument. This consisted of obtaining the difference between each respondent's M and F scale scores, converting the result to a $t$ score, and using the mean and standard deviation of a norm group in computing the $t$ ratio. However, following analysis by Spence, Helmreich, and Stapp (1975) and Strahan (1975), Bem (1977) acknowledged the utility of using a median split technique suggested by Spence et al., which takes into consideration the absolute level of the individual's scores on each scale. This is accomplished by first calculating each person's mean F and M scores, then classifying them as follows. Those above the group (or norm) median on the F scale and below on the M scale are called Feminine, those above the median on M and below on F are Masculine, those above on both M and F are Androgynous, and those below on both are Undifferentiated. The scoring controversy is discussed in a later section of this chapter, but here let us mention that Spence and Helmreich (1979b) have noted that the median split technique may have a higher congruence with the multidimensionality of M and F scores.

From the beginning, Bem has sought to establish behavioral manifestations of BSRI categories. This has led to research designed to relate scale responses to, as Worell (1978) has put it, "something else." Studies by Bem (Bem, 1975; Bem et al., 1976; Bem & Lenney, 1976) examining behavioral congruence with BSRI classification have been used to establish the instrument's validity. Subjects were classified according to their BSRI responses and observed in their interactions with a kitten (Bem & Lenney, 1976), a human baby, or a lonely fellow student (Bem et al., 1976). Other behavioral correlates examined were the performance of cross-sex activities such as pounding a nail or rolling yarn into a ball. Bem et al. (1976) conclude from their results that Androgynous individuals, male and female, "are capable of being both independent and nurturant, both instrumental and expressive, both masculine and feminine" (p. 1022). In contrast, sex-typed individuals (Masculine males and Feminine females) showed a reluctance to engage in cross-sex behavior. Bem et al. suggest that sex typing restricts effective behavioral functioning in either the expressive or instrumental domain. Despite these claims, the data did not conform consistently to expectations. Feminine females were not nurturant and expressive across situations. This may be due to the instrumental behavior required even in primarily expressive situations (Bem et al., 1976), or it may be that Feminine women's ratings reflect a socially desirable response bias rather than their true characteristics (Kelly & Worell, 1977). Another possibility, of course, may be that there are minimal amounts of behavioral congruence with what is measured on the BSRI because the instrument taps something else other than masculinity and femininity or only one facet of it.

The development of the PAQ by Spence et al. (1974, 1975) was accomplished in two phases. This began with a replication and extension of the work by Rosenkrantz, Vogel, Bee, Broverman, and Broverman (1968), whose pool of items came from student nominations of characteristics differentiating men and women. The original investigation obtained ratings of typical adult males and females as well as the ideal individual on each item. Spence et al. asked college students to rate the typical male and female adult or the typical male and female college student or the ideal male and female individual on each item. Finally, these students rated themselves. The 55 items subsequently selected for the PAQ reflected sex-stereotype ratings in that both male and female respondents produced significant differences for the ratings of each sex. Self-ratings on all 55 items also showed significant sex differences in the stereotyped direction. Further, the PAQ items appear to be representative of socially positive characteristics because ideal ratings were also in the stereotyped direction. A short form of the PAQ has been developed and consists similarly of three 8-item scales, the basis for item elimination having been part-whole correlations between items and total subscale score. These three subscales on both the long and short form of the PAQ include Masculinity (M), Femininity (F), and Masculinity-Femininity (M-F). Items on the M scale are considered to be socially desirable attributes for both sexes, but attributes that males are believed to possess to a greater degree. The same is true for females on the F scale. Items on the M-F scale, on the other hand, are those judged to be socially desirable for one sex but not for the other. For example, aggressiveness is considered to be a desirable trait in males, but nonaggressiveness is desirable in females. The underlying conception on the M-F scale, then, is a bipolar one in contrast to the M and F scales on the PAQ as well as the BSRI. Similar to the BSRI, the M and F scales on the PAQ are essentially independent in ratings by both men and women. The M-F scale is moderately positively related to M and substantially negatively related to F, thus providing further substantiation of its bipolar nature.

Unlike Bem who has appeared confident that the BSRI would prove to be a broad measure of M and F, Spence and her colleagues have remained extremely cautious in making broad claims for their instrument. They emphasize (Spence & Helmreich, 1979a) that the PAQ M and F scales measure domains rather narrow in scope, a sense of "agency" on the M scale and a sense of "communion" on the F scale. Spence and Helmreich (1978) cite Bakan (1966) as providing the theoretical basis for defining these modalities. Agency, identified with the male, involves self-concerns (self-assertion, self-protection), while communion, associated with the female, involves a concern for and being with others. The scales are also related to Parsons and Bales's (1955) concept of instrumental and expressive traits in masculine and feminine characterizations, respectively.

Spence and her colleagues have examined the relationship of the PAQ to an attitude measure, the Attitude toward Women Scale (AWS) (Spence & Helmreich, 1972), which assesses beliefs regarding the rights and roles of women in society. Subjects' stereotype scores on the PAQ (ratings of others) were moderately correlated with AWS ratings, those perceiving large differences in the roles of women and men having higher stereotype ratings. Spence and Helmreich (1978) speculate that perhaps this relationship may stem from a tendency by traditionally oriented individuals to perceive exaggerated sex differences as a justification for this outlook. The converse would also apply. Examination of the relationship of self-report scores with AWS ratings were low, although the correlations were in the expected direction (Spence et al., 1975; Spence & Helmreich, 1978). The authors suggest that the psychological characteristics of masculinity and femininity are not related to societal roles.

A different picture emerges, however, when PAQ scores are examined in relationship to self-esteem and social competence as measured by the Texas Social Behavior Inventory (TSBI) (Helmreich et al., 1974). High positive correlations were found for both males and females with M scale scores. Lower but substantial correlations were evident in F scale scores with self-esteem for both sexes. Further analyses revealed that Androgynous subjects were highest in self-esteem, followed by Masculine, Feminine, and Undifferentiated individuals. This result directly contradicts traditional tenets that assume that cross-sex characteristics are inimical to adjustment and psychological well-being (Spence & Helmreich, 1978).

MEASURE APPLIED TO CHILDREN

Research into children's gender biases is sparse. The few studies that do exist serve to point up the difficulties inherent in dealing with younger subjects, particularly in an area remarkable for its lack of operational definitions.

We have made earlier mention of the study by Sears et al. (1965) in which stereotypic responses were examined in a number of areas. Williams et al. (1975) also explored children's stereotypes, adapting the Sex Stereotype Measure for use with younger subjects. Terms were simplified and similar adjectives grouped together in story form, resulting in, for example, to cover the male adjective constellation "aggressive, assertive, forceful, tough": "One of these people is a bully. They are always pushing people around and getting into fights. Which person gets into fights?" (p. 636). With pictures as aids, 12 stories for female and 12 for male stereotypes were developed; subjects were kindergarten through fourth-grade children. Three scores were computed for each respondent based on the number of correct responses given (female stereotype sub-score, male stereotype subscore, and total stereotype subscore). Williams et al. found that even by the fourth grade, children do not yet have full knowledge of sex-role stereotypes. Further, male stereotypes are learned earlier by both girls and boys; the researchers conjectured that this may be due to the greater number of components in the male stereotype that involve overt behavior or to the fact that little-boy stereotypes are closer to adult male stereotypes than little-girl and adult female stereotypes.

As part of the assessment battery of a project to introduce a nonsexist curriculum in kindergarten through ninth-grade classes, Guttentag and Bray (1976, 1977) developed a semantic differential instrument to measure sex stereotypes and psychological sex. Items included five female and five male socially desirable stereotyped attributes as well as five undesirable attributes for each sex. In addition, two neutral desirable and two neutral undesirable characteristics filled out the scale. Children rated the items on a 5-point continuum, one pole containing a socially desirable adjective for one sex and a socially undesirable adjective for the other sex. Concepts rated included "self," "real girls," "real boys," "ideal girls," and "ideal boys." Guttentag and Bray report no psychometric data, nor do they explain the scales' development. Results indicated that fifth-grade children tended to stereotype the opposite sex more than themselves and girls tended to rate both sexes more androgynously (attributing socially desirable adjectives to both sexes).

Several problems specific to the measurement of sex-role stereotypes and psychological sex in children are reflected in the above studies and were serious considerations in our own research. The first is the imposition upon children of adult conceptions of what constitutes a stereotype; we have no idea of whether this procedure is valid, yet both sets of researchers above adapted adult measures for use with children. Williams et al. and Guttentag and Bray took items similar to those used in stereotype ratings by college students. In the former study, fourth-grade students were found to still have incomplete knowledge of stereotypes, yet we really have no way of knowing whether this is actually the case or whether children's stereotypes comprise characteristics different from those of college-aged adults.

The second difficulty in measuring sex-role bias in children is the abstract nature of many stereotypic attributes. Terms such as leadership and sensitive represent difficult concepts for youngsters to deal with, and their inability to correctly apply such terms may produce low reliabilities and theoretically inexplicable results. The Guttentag and Bray instrument actually contains many of these abstract attributes, while Williams et al. attempted to solve the problem through the development of story situations representing an abstract concept. However, this strategy may have confounded the results. Recall that male stereotypes contained more behavioral components and were also better known by children in the study. It may be that the difficulty of converting the more abstract female stereotypes into story form resulted in poorer items on the female scale. Male stereotypes may not be learned earlier; higher sub-scale scores in this case may be due to children's clearer comprehension of the questions asked.

Yet another difficult problem involves the sex of the experimenter, but the reason for possible confounding effects is both startling and intriguing. One might suspect that children would respond differently to women than to men, and this in fact has been found as an effect in stereotype ratings. In the Williams et al. study, older children of both sexes responded with more "correct" stereotypic answers when the examiner was male rather than female. Maccoby and Jacklin (1974) have discussed the greater degree of enforcement of the sex-role standard by fathers than by mothers, and subjects in the Williams et al. study may have been responding to an expectation that the male would sanction more stereotypic responses. Williams et al. cite the knowledge versus the expression of sex stereotypes, and correlate this to the sex of the examiner—expression being greatest with the male. However, this may bring into question from another vantage point their conclusion regarding incomplete knowledge of stereotypes by the fourth grade. Again, we cannot be sure whether knowledge in these children was actually incomplete or whether they were merely responding to expectations, and if so, to what degree.

We were well aware of some of the pitfalls we were facing in our initial "Freestyle" research; we also encountered other problems we did not anticipate, such as the low reliabilities in self-ratings of personality attributes in comparison with ratings of others (see Chapter 5). This probably reflects the concrete-abstract labeling problem in that children may have learned by rote stereotype labels applying to "most girls" and "most boys" but find difficulty in evaluating themselves in regard to, say, "shy" or "friendly."

## ISSUES AND CONSIDERATIONS
## REGARDING SEX-ROLE SCALES

Are we moving toward yet another reconceptualization of masculinity and femininity? The literature reads like a mystery novel but one still in the process of completion. What are the clues and where do they lead us? In this section we review current thought and evaluate our position.

Issues currently under discussion regarding the conceptualization and measurement of masculinity and femininity, including androgyny, include both the implications of the various scoring methods in the definition of androgyny, and the psychometric adequacy of the scales themselves.

### Scoring: The Operational Definition
### of Androgyny

In assessing relationships between psychological sex and other traits or behaviors, the scoring method becomes critical whereby M and F scales join to yield the category "Androgynous." As Pedhazur and Tetenbaum (1979) note, Bem has never explicitly defined androgyny except to say that it is the combination in one individual of the positive characteristics of both sexes. The only specific definition has been methodological, a difference (or balance) score between Masculine and Feminine BSRI scores. Spence and Helmreich (1978, 1979a) have expressed their reticence to use the term androgyny and employ it only as a convenient label for those individuals high in both Masculinity and Femininity on the PAQ. Following the Spence et al. (1975) suggestion that a median split (absolute) method would take into account the level of M and F in categorizing individuals and would yield, in addition to the sex-typed categories, both an Androgynous classification for those scoring high on both M and F and an Undifferentiated classification for those low on both scales, Bem's (1977) evaluation of the method took a strictly empirical tack (Pedhazur & Tetenbaum, 1979): Classify subjects according to median splits and look for differences between Androgynous and Undifferentiated individuals. Finding a few, Bem deems the new method a valuable one. Unfortunately for either view, as Pedhazur and Tetenbaum as well as Locksley and Colten (1979) point out, Bem is not able to specify when and how these two classifications of people will differ on further traits or behaviors.

The absolute method has also come under attack, however. Pedhazur and Tetenbaum (1979) point out its crudeness—the fact that scores close together at the middle of the scale may result in differential classification and that the manner in which individuals are classified depends in part upon the group to which they belong. A detailed analysis has been presented by Spence and Helmreich (1979b) in which they evaluated the relative advantages of the various scoring methods proposed. They find multiple regression perhaps the least satisfactory, despite its recommendation by Bem (1977) and Worell (1978). Spence and Helmreich's reservations derive from the difficulty they encountered in providing a theoretical base for significant interaction terms. They recommend that the researcher in this area avoid multiple regression unless a prior hypothesis can be specified for interactions between the variables involved. The relative advantages and disadvantages of the other scoring methods are a bit more equivocal, theoretically at least.

Spence and Helmreich (1979b) present specific analyses demonstrating their points, and the reader is referred to their paper for greater detail. For our purposes here, the important factors are these: that there is no one mathematical model appropriate for all data sets, that precision in any model is lacking so that individual predictions are not advisable, and that the researcher should carefully assess the fit of the various mathematical models to each new set of variables. The median split method may be most appropriate when the individual correlations among the variables are linear and their combinations additive, as, for example, the finding that Androgynous subjects had the highest self-esteem scores, followed successively by Masculine, Feminine, and Undifferentiated individuals. The balance method, on the other hand, may be more appropriate when the relationships between M and F and the other variables under scrutiny are not linear. Spence and Helmreich, however, specify no situations in which this may be the case.

They also evaluate Orlofsky, Aslin, and Ginsburg's (1977) "difference/median" method, a combination of absolute and balance methods, which employs Bem's original difference technique to obtain sex-typed and balanced classifications but then divides the balanced group into two via a median split, yielding Androgynous and Undifferentiated subjects. According to Spence and Helmreich, this method suffers from the a priori theoretical bias of Bem's balance technique, that M and F contribute equally but in opposite directions. The primary difference in actual subject classification between the Orlofsky et al. method and the absolute method is that some Androgynous individuals would be labeled sex-typed with the Spence and Helmreich technique.

## Psychometric Considerations

Several aspects of the PAQ and the BSRI's psychometric characteristics have been under criticism of late, primarily in the areas of validity, social desirability of the items, and factor structure.

The establishment of the construct validity of the M and F scales has proceeded slowly. Validation has come primarily via predictive validity in the case of the BSRI or through the establishment of relationships with other, nonsex-related variables in the case of the PAQ (Locksley & Colten, 1979). The question of validity necessarily has different implications for the BSRI and the PAQ. Bem has consistently described her instrument as a measure of masculinity and femininity, although like the PAQ it contains primarily instrumental and expressive traits. On the other hand, Spence and her colleagues have cautioned that the PAQ does not measure masculinity and femininity as broad concepts but rather as the instrumental and expressive traits that represent the "essential core" of these (Helmreich, Spence, & Wilhelm, in press; Spence & Helmreich, 1979a). Further, as Spence and Helmreich (1979a) point out, the entire question of validity rests upon the theory behind the scales themselves. A failure by Bem to find a strong relationship between BSRI categories and behavior would mean lowered validity from her perspective but support for Spence and Helmreich's theory, which posits a weak relationship between the two. While this discrepancy in theoretical positions creates confusion regarding the validity question, it nevertheless illustrates the viewpoints and approaches by researchers in the field.

Analyses have been lacking that specifically center on the social desirability aspects of the BSRI and the PAQ. However, a detailed examination of the former instrument by Pedhazur and Tetenbaum (1979) resulted in two findings: that social desirability does appear to be a factor in BSRI ratings with extremely small differences between males and females on some items and that the Feminine scale contains some items that are socially undesirable for both sexes. The authors attribute these difficulties to the strict-ly empirical derivation of the BSRI, a charge not easily levied against Spence and her colleagues, who have exercised both theoreti-cal as well as empirical considerations in the development of the PAQ.

This contrast between instruments is reflected in factor ana-lytic results, which for the BSRI generally yield a four-factor solu-tion (Gaudreau, 1977; Pedhazur & Tetenbaum, 1979) with differing factor patterns for males and females (Pedhazur & Tetenbaum, 1979; Wakefield, Sasek, Friedman, & Bowden, 1976). A factor analysis of the PAQ, on the other hand, reflects its theoretical basis (Helm-reich et al., in press). Two factors were found for each sex, one instrumental and one expressive, with similar results from three different samples.

In the face of current criticism, Bem (1979) offers two strate-gies. The first is to shorten the BSRI, eliminating problematic items (those measuring "masculinity" and "femininity" directly, those feminine items with negative desirability, and others). The second is to negate the concept of androgyny as a viable and useful tool in psychological research. Rather, Bem proposes a "gender schema," which exists in children by 1 or 2 years of age. This is a cognitive construct, one involving awareness of both biological sex and cultural mores. Individuals vary in "gender polarity" or how much they believe the sexes to differ. Therefore, sex-typed as compared with androgynous people hold different beliefs regarding the similarity of men and women, and these beliefs are reflected in their own self-descriptions and behavior. No longer does Bem see her primary research focus as the measurement of how much mas-culinity or femininity individuals possess but, rather, as assess-ment of the degree to which people use gender-related information for processing data and how much they perceive the sexes to differ. Thus, Bem regards androgyny as a temporary construct; as its mes-sage is accepted by society, the distinction between masculine and feminine traits will disappear and with it the concept of androgyny.

Spence and Helmreich (1979a) hold a different view, that an-drogyny exists in many forms and that these need to be examined. Rather than reject the entire concept, they suggest that gender-related components of psychological functioning be measured so that their interrelationships may be determined.


IMPLICATIONS FOR "FREESTYLE"

When one reviews the original documentation leading to the TV CAP, it is evident that a much more simple concept of sex-role stereotyping was in mind than one with the complexities just reviewed.

In the mid-1970s, the initial concerns for developing materials to intervene in children's stereotyping were mainly the degree to which much of the work on adult stereotyping might carry over to children and what the implications would be for a change process. The book by Guttentag and Bray (1976), which describes an intervention project with grade school children, provides an excellent example of such practical concerns. It is also an example of the calm before the storm, so to speak. There was little questioning of whether simple bipolar measures of stereotypes would be sufficient, and stereotyping itself was assumed to be a rather global process. It is as if intervention materials could be targeted for a child's central sex-role biases, much as if sex-role stereotyping were a fundamental mediator in the child's behavior.

Our own approach was not so different from Guttentag and Bray's at the outset. Despite some signs of the impending storm over conceptualization and measurement of sex-role stereotyping, the assumption of stereotypes as a global phenomenon seemed useful to us. We were, however, not satisfied with the evidence that the scales used to date were all that applicable to children. Above all, we took the position that if we were dealing with sex-role stereotyping as a global concept, we should be able to find evidence of it in different concept domains. Moreover, we should find evidence of relations among these domains. If a child had a strong female bias and this were a global concept, ratings of personalities, activity interests, occupations, and the like should show some degree of correlation. Accordingly, replications of scales heretofore used with children and our attempts to see relationships of stereotyping across domains occupied us as one major initial phase of our original research. These studies are reported in Chapters 4 through 7.

As will be seen, however, we, like others, found problems with these earlier conceptualizations and scales and, as a consequence, altered the course of our own work.

# 3

## HOW TELEVISION COULD
## INFLUENCE SEX-ROLE LEARNING

If real life abounds in sex-role stereotyping, television confirms if not exaggerates these biases by portraying markedly more males than females in programs, by showing males in dominant roles, by having women more often victims of violence, and with only a few exceptions, by showing that the career world is a male one. It is not unusual, therefore, that most of the research literature that relates sex-role stereotyping to television is of the content analytic type. This has often been researched and continues to be monitored. Although we review such research in this chapter, the content analytic studies lack the significant component as to how (or if) television viewing may affect sex-role stereotyping. Common sense would suggest that if four to six hours of a child's day were spent in viewing television stereotypes, this would have a concomitant effect upon attitudes and behaviors regarding sex roles. Yet the content analytic studies cannot alone bridge the gap to confirm effects, and this is a critical shortcoming too often overlooked when they are used as criticism of contemporary broadcast practices.

Another category of study, one that is addressed to the relationship between television viewing and effects on behavior, we call correlational. The strategy in such studies is to relate the amount of time spent with television—viewing frequencies or frequency of viewing a particular type of content—with the variables of effects on attitudes or behavior. These studies are not experimental in the sense that television content and exposure are manipulated as an independent variable, all situational variables controlled, and the effects studies as a true dependent variable. Instead, they are more descriptive in nature, leaving whatever correlations are found subject to problems of confounding or ambiguity. Nevertheless, such studies have been, and are, a continuing source of insight into the probable effects of television upon children.

Both the content analytic and the correlational studies can be criticized in the quantity-versus-quality argument in theorizing about the effects of television on children. Are children's attitudes and behaviors affected by different exposure frequencies to characterizations, performers, plots, and the like? Or are they more affected by the qualities of these factors—for example, by successful characters, attractive performers, or motivating plots? Experimental studies are especially useful in this respect. Here the quality as well as the quantity of television exposure can be manipulated, other relevant variables controlled, and the effects on specific attitudes and behaviors studied. Despite the precision of experimental research designs, they remain a distinct minority in television research. They are costly. Moreover, what they gain in precision (being conducted in a laboratory-type environment) they lose in representativeness to our real world of viewing television while stretched out on the family room carpet.

Finally, there are studies that although not directly involving television do suggest ways of conceptualizing how the medium could affect sex-role learning. We review several generalizations from such studies, most of which are compatible with generalizations culled from the psychological research literature on sex-role stereotyping discussed in Chapter 2.

## PRIOR RESEARCH

### Content Analytic Studies

Undoubtedly, the most widely researched aspect of the relationship among children, television, and sex-role stereotyping is the nature of sex roles in television content seen by children. Numerous content analytic studies show that traditional sex roles completely permeate the television programs children see. Women are underrepresented in virtually every aspect of the television schedule and every kind of programming seen by children. Women fill only about a third of the roles in prime time (Sternglanz & Serbin, 1974; Tedesco, 1974; U.S. Civil Rights Commission, 1977). The percentage is even lower on Saturday mornings (Gerbner & Gross, 1974; Levinson, 1973; McArthur & Eizen, 1976; Streicher, 1974). Public television is also relatively lacking in female roles. Only 15 percent of the characters in adult-oriented Public Broadcasting System (PBS) programs are female (Cantor, 1977), and males outnumber females by as much as two to one in PBS children's programs (Cantor, 1977; Corporation for Public Broadcasting, 1975). Educational programming is not immune (Dohram, 1975). Neither is the ever-present commercial. The vast majority of announcers on commercials are men (Courtney & Whipple, 1974; Dominick & Rauch, 1972). Men also fill 63 percent of the roles in public service announcements seen on Saturday mornings (Scheutz & Sprafkin, 1978).

Of equal concern is the nature of the sex-role portrayals on television. In quality as well as quantity, women are clearly second-class citizens. Only about one-third of the women are employed in prime time, compared with two-thirds of the men (McNeil, 1975; Tedesco, 1974). When women are employed, they are most frequently found in traditional female occupations such as nurse, secretary, maid, or entertainer (Seggar & Wheeler, 1973). In general, females are in marital, romantic, or family roles, while men are found in professional, powerful, prestigious roles (Gerbner, 1972; Long & Simon, 1974).

Women seldom get the better of men in their interactions on television. Men tend to dominate women twice as often as women dominate men (Lemon, 1978). When the interactions are violent ones, women are the victimized, men are the victimizers (Gerbner, Gross, Jackson-Beeck, Jeffries-Fox, & Signorielli, 1978; Tedesco, 1974). Men give and receive more approvals and disapprovals than women on Saturday morning television (Nolan, Galst, & White, 1977), further indicating that it is the men on television who hold the power.

The sexes also differ in their personalities and characteristic patterns of behavior. Men on Saturday morning television are more active, problem solving, autonomous, and discordant than the women (McArthur & Eizen, 1976). In television programs most often seen by children, women are less aggressive and constructive than men but more deferent and succorant (Sternglanz & Serbin, 1974). Busby's (1974) study of the sex-role standard in 20 network cartoon shows revealed women to be less ambitious, competitive, adventuresome, and so on, and more affectionate, sensitive, and romantic than men. In short, female and male characters on television most often seen by children generally conform to the characteristics of their traditional sex roles.

Commercials add to the problem. In commercials women hold only about 33 percent of the visible professional jobs and 10 percent of the managerial jobs but 100 percent of the clerk-typist jobs (Maracek, Piliavin, Fitzsimmons, Krogh, Leader, & Trudell, 1978). Women tend to appear only in commercials for feminine products and in domestic settings. Overall, four-fifths of the women in commercials are in domestic roles or subservient occupations (Dominick & Rauch, 1972). Commercials on Saturday morning incorporate similar biases (Verna, 1975). Even their production styles betray subtle stereotyping. Commercials for boys products are marked by activity, varied scenes, numerous cuts, loud sound tracks, male narrators, and aggressive behavior. Commercials for girls feature frequent fades and dissolves, background music, and female narrators (Verna, 1975; Welch, Huston-Stein, Wright, & Plehal, 1979).

Despite the vitality of the women's movement throughout the early 1970s, there is no evidence that this has been reflected in changing sex roles on television. The frequency and content of women's roles were about the same in the mid-1970s as they were in the early part of the decade (O'Donnell & O'Donnell, 1978).

Correlational Studies

Correlational studies provide limited supportive evidence for a "cultivation hypothesis" by showing the relationship of heavy television viewership to traditional sex-role preferences. In a study of preschoolers, Beuf (1974) found that 76 percent of heavy viewers, compared with 50 percent of moderate viewers, expressed an interest in occupations traditional for their sex. Freuh and McGhee (1975) found that high television viewers exhibited more traditional sex-role preferences than did moderate viewers in kindergarten and the second, fourth, and sixth grades. Among boys but not among girls, Gross and Jeffries-Fox (1978) found a significant but low correlation ($r$ = .19) between television viewing and sexist answers to questions about women's roles.

However, some serious limitations apply to these studies. The Beuf results are based on an extremely small sample size ($n$ = 63). The exact numbers on which the comparisons between heavy and light viewers are based are not discernible from her report but are, perhaps, so small that even the 26 percent difference between the two groups may not be highly significant. The Freuh and McGhee study also employed a small sample. They used the it Scale for children, a measure that appears to be an invalid measure of sex-role preference (Mischel, 1970), particularly among older children (Kohlberg, 1966). In the Gross and Jeffries-Fox study, correlations between television viewership and questions about women's roles were dramatically reduced after controlling for intelligence.

In their "cultivation" hypothesis, Gerbner and Gross (1976) hold that the television medium gradually affects heavy viewers by consistently portraying an alternate world view over a number of years, which ultimately reinforces and cultivates the world view of the audience.

As it is, the predominantly traditional sex-role portrayals in television content may actually cultivate resistance to change in sex roles by discrediting, isolating, and undercutting the few exemplars of change that appear in the medium (Gerbner, 1978). On this basis, there is little reason to hope that any single counterstereotypical intervention could have much impact at all.

Correlational studies fail to establish the direction of causation. In this case, a plausible alternative explanation is that children with traditional sex roles may prefer to watch television more than those with nontraditional sex roles. There may be patterns of selective exposure and perception at work that better explain the results. Cultivation theory equivocates somewhat on this point. On the one hand, it is claimed that selective exposure is part and parcel of the cultivation effect (Gerbner et al., 1978). On the other hand, it is also claimed that television is also watched in ritualistic fashion without respect to the content (Gerbner & Gross, 1974).

Even if one assumes that ritualistic exposure to sex-typed television content cultivates traditional sex roles, there is still the question of how deep-seated such effects may be. Are they really the end product of years of exposure to a sex-stereotyped alternate reality? Another possible explanation is that the relationship between heavy viewing and sex-role preference is merely the result of recent exposure to television. In that case, the impact of a single series—or even a single program—might be considerable. It should be noted that the measures of television exposure employed in studies of cultivation effects are based on relatively recent exposure to the medium in the preceding days or weeks. At best, they are retrospective self-reports of viewing in the past, which may be biased by recent viewing behavior.

On the other hand, one could argue that the very pervasiveness of traditional sex roles in television may be the basis of their undoing. The presentation of nontraditional sex roles might have high information value and attract the attention of the audience. Such portrayals might even set an agenda for social change (cf. Roberts, 1971). The mechanism of observational learning (Bandura, 1969; Comstock, Chafee, Katzman, McCombs, & Roberts, 1978; Liebert, 1972) explains the acquisition and performance of novel behaviors shown on television. Presumably, nontraditional sex-role behaviors can be learned as readily as any others. We can invoke this mechanism to explain how a few nontraditional portrayals might alter children's tendencies to perform sex-typed behavior.

In this vein, Miller and Reeves (1976) found that exposure to females in counterstereotypical occupations impacted upon corresponding real-life perceptions. Elementary school children who could identify select counterstereotypical female characters on

television thought it was appropriate for females to be in the characters' occupations more than did children who could not identify
the characters. For one of the five female leads tested, children's
perceptions of the numbers of females in the corresponding real-
life occupation were also affected. Apparently, the more prominent the character was, the stronger the counterstereotypical effect.

These results challenge the assumptions of the cultivation
hypothesis in that they suggest that a small number of nontraditional
portrayals can counter the predominantly traditional sex-role bias
of the medium. The Miller and Reeves study holds out some hope
that the creation of prominent, counterstereotypical roles might
alter children's beliefs about real-life sex roles. However, the
correlational design of this study leaves open the possibility that
the results reflect patterns of selective exposure or recall, just as
they do in studies that support the cultivation hypothesis. Moreover, the Miller and Reeves study only found effects on sex-role
stereotypes with respect to the perceived appropriateness of adult
occupations. Beliefs about the distribution of the sexes in real-
world occupations were mostly unchanged.


Experimental Studies

Experimental studies can rule out the selective exposure explanation. Atkin and Miller (1975) showed grade school children
commercials that portrayed women in traditionally male occupations.
Children who saw these especially prepared commercials were more
likely to believe that the occupations were appropriate for women
than children who saw other commercials.

Pingree (1978) showed third- and eighth-grade children commercials depicting either traditional or nontraditional occupational
roles for women under three conditions of perceived reality.
Children were instructed that the characters were either all real
people or only actors or were given no instruction (in a control
group). Children's perception of the reality of television and their
attitudes about women were the dependent measures. The perceived
reality manipulation was successful. However, the attitude change
results were very mixed. In the group that received no instructions
about perceived reality, those who saw nontraditional commercials
had more nontraditional attitudes about women than those who saw
the traditional commercials. However, among eighth-grade boys,
the reverse effect was observed. Eighth-grade boys who saw the
nontraditional commercials were more traditional in their attitudes
than those who saw the traditional commercials. There was no
interaction between perceived reality and attitudes about women.

Pingree explains these results by noting that the control (no perceived reality instruction) may not have been comparable with the rest of the sample. The children in the control group watched less television than other children, and on the (circular) assumption that television causes sex-role stereotyping (after Beuf, 1974; Freuh & McGhee, 1975), they may have already been relatively nontraditional themselves. The brief (5-minute) exposure may not have been sufficient to induce differences in that group. Since the groups in the study were not randomly assigned (Pingree, 1976) and no pretest was given, it is in fact quite possible that all of Pingree's results were the result of preexisting between-group differences in attitudes about women. Even taking the results at face value, the findings that older boys became more stereotyped in their attitudes toward women flies in the face of the assumption that the simple portrayal of counterstereotypical roles will change stereotypes. These results remind us that such efforts may boomerang if they are not carefully designed.

O'Bryant and Corder-Bolz (1978) performed a similer experiment with elementary school children. They showed the children especially designed commercials portraying women in jobs traditionally held by men. In this case, experimental groups were randomly assigned and a pretest was given to control for initial between-group differences. Following exposure to the commercials, girls were more likely to prefer nontraditional occupations than girls who saw commercials with women in traditional occupations. However, boys who saw the nontraditional commercials were actually less likely to prefer traditionally male jobs, perhaps as a result of seeing only females in such jobs. All children were likely to consider traditionally male jobs more appropriate for females after seeing females in those jobs.

Flerx et al. (1976) showed films featuring egalitarian (as opposed to sex-stereotyped) portrayals to kindergarten children over a seven-day period. They examined pre-post changes in children's acceptance of nontraditional occupations for women, nontraditional play activities for children, and beliefs about the relative intelligence and affect-expressiveness of men and women. Posttest scores on the first three measures were significantly higher than on the pretest, an effect that persisted in a 1-week delayed posttest. Although the results were significant for both sexes, they were not as strong for boys and they were for girls.

In all, studies that explicitly tested the effects of nontraditional television portrayals on children's sex-role concepts produced somewhat mixed results. In two studies perceptions about the appropriateness of adult jobs for women were affected (Atkin & Miller, 1975). This finding extends to children's own sex-role preferences relative to adult jobs (O'Bryant & Corder-Bolz, 1978) and to their stereotypes of adult male household roles and childhood activities (Flerx et al., 1976). Pingree's study, while purporting to be about "attitudes" concerning women, actually assessed children's beliefs about the appropriateness of traditional women's roles (for example, agreement with the statement, "Married women should stay home and be housewives and mothers"). It is thus seen as a parallel to the O'Bryant and Corder-Bolz study and one that introduces one null finding and one reverse finding—that nontraditional portrayals may, for some children, strengthen traditional sex-role beliefs. This is a reminder that simple role reversal may have its pitfalls as an "intervention" strategy and may be relatively ineffective among boys. The studies leave open the question of whether television can be used to alter the more immediate effects of sex-role stereotyping on children, since all three focus on adult, rather than childhood, sex roles. Flerx et al. (1976) found that perceptions of the sex appropriateness of childhood activities could be altered but did not examine effects on children's own attitudes toward sex-typed behavior or their intentions to engage in such behavior.

## The Observational Learning Perspectives

In the extensive literature on the observational learning of sex-role behavior, a useful distinction is made between the acquisition of and the performance of imitative behavior (Bandura, 1969). Acquisition refers to the information processing of modeling stimuli into images and words for storage in memory. Stimuli coded in this fashion serve as symbolic mediators for response retrieval and reproduction. The stored symbols mediate the performance of, or the actual reproduction of, the matching behavior.

If television is to be used to promote observational learning—in this case, the learning of nontraditional sex-role behaviors—a necessary first step is the acquisition of the behavior by viewers. That is, children must attend to and recognize the modeling sequence and retain the modeling events in memory on a long-term basis before they can actually reproduce the behavior themselves.

There is evidence that elementary school children selectively recall media content that is congruent with traditional sex-roles (Maccoby & Wilson, 1957). Children generally recall more of the behavior of actors of their own sex than of actors of the opposite sex. However, when sex-inappropriate behavior is involved, such as when females act aggressively or males act romantically, children tend not to recall the counterstereotypical behavior of members of their own sex. Children may use sex-role stereotypes as an organizational framework, recalling more stereotyped traits of male and female characters than counterstereotypical traits. Feminine traits of male actors are particularly hard for children to recall (Koblinsky, Cruse, & Sugawara, 1978).

Some studies with younger children offer exceptions to this generalization. For example, McArthur and Eizen (1976) found that there was greater recall of the behavior of the same sex than of an opposite sex model, regardless of the sex type of the behavior among preschoolers. Grusec and Brinker (1972) found that the masculinity or femininity of a behavior did not affect first- and second-grade children's ability to recall it. As Slaby and Frey (1975) point out, it is possible that younger children have not as yet achieved a constant concept of their gender identity ("gender constancy") and so may not be as susceptible to selective recall.

There may also be sex differences in the selective acquisition of counterstereotypical behavior. Boys are more likely to exhibit selective recall than girls (Bryan & Luria, 1978; Grusec & Brinker, 1972). This effect may be attributable to the more rigid restrictions and higher value placed on the male sex role (McArthur & Eizen, 1976).

The sex appropriateness of behavior, rather than the sex appropriateness of the model, may also prompt selective acquisition. Bryan and Luria (1978) found that both 5- to 6-year-olds and 9- to 10-year-olds recalled more same-sex tasks than opposite-sex tasks regardless of the sex of the model.

Selective recall of counterstereotypical behavior may in turn be the result of selective attention. Maccoby, Wilson, and Burton (1958) found that college-age boys watched the male leads and girls, the female leads in films. Sprafkin and Liebert (1978) found much the same for first- and second-grade children. They also found that selective attention applied to the sex typedness of the actor's behavior. For example, girls attended 78 percent of the time to female characters exhibiting sex-typed behavior but only 52 percent of the time to females performing nonsex-typed behavior. However, Bryan and Luria (1978) found no evidence of selective attention when alpha blocking, rather than observation of eye movements, was used as the measure of attention. Bryan and Luria speculated that previous findings about selective attention effects may have been a consequence of failing to measure attention precisely and validly.

A final explanation for the conflicting findings on selective acquisition is offered by Slaby and Frey (1975). They note that experiments on the acquisition of sex-typed behavior fail to determine whether the subjects themselves perceive the behaviors or the models to be sex appropriate. Selective acquisition should only take place when models are seen as sex inappropriate in the eye of the beholder. To date, no research on the acquisition of sex-role behavior (including Slaby and Frey's) has included observer perceptions as an explanatory variable.

Social learning theory predicts that selective acquisition will carry over to selective performance. That is, if children do not acquire a counterstereotypical behavior due to selective attention or recall, it will be impossible for them to perform it. Even if nontraditional sex-role behaviors can be acquired from television, will they be performed? Or will societal norms inhibit their expression?

Beginning with the early studies of observational learning by Bandura, Ross, and Ross (1963) and Bandura (1965), sex differences were found in imitative behavior. In these and many other studies in which the sex of the model and the sex of the observer were varied, male observers were found to imitate male models more than female observers did. Other studies found that girls imitated female models more than boys did. However, a more common finding was that boys and girls were equally likely to imitate male or female models (cf. Maccoby & Jacklin, 1974).

Barkley et al. (1977) found in this array of conflicting findings reason to believe that the sex appropriateness of the modeled behavior, rather than the sex of the model alone, might well be the crucial factor. That is, boys would always imitate male-typed behavior (such as, aggression) regardless of the sex of the model. Upon manipulating the sex appropriateness of the behavior, Barkley et al. found that girls tended to imitate female behavior more than masculine behavior regardless of the biological sex of the model. The corresponding effect only tended toward significance for boys. However, in the case of the boys, there is no assurance that the male subjects perceived the play behavior to be sex appropriate for them. Although the play was vigorous and aggressive and involved male-typed toys (such as, a truck), there was a strong fantasy element in which the models imagined themselves to be a (GI Joe) doll. The strong fantasy aspect of the stimulus sequence may have reduced its perceived sex appropriateness. Perhaps imagining oneself to be a doll (even GI Joe) is not a highly masculine thing to do. The modeling sequence, taken as a whole, may not have been sex appropriate in the eyes of the male subjects.

On the other hand, an experiment by Wolf (1973) suggests that it is the biological sex of the model, rather than the sex typedness of the behavior, that is the dominant factor. Wolf found that boys imitated a sex-inappropriate behavior (playing with a toy oven) more from a same-sex model than from an opposite-sex model. The same effect only tended toward significance for girls, however. The latter null finding may have been due to the fact that girls found the same-sex model no more attractive than the opposite-sex model, while boys found the model of their own sex significantly more attractive.

When Montemayor (1974) manipulated the sex appropriateness of a task by clearly labeling it as for boys or for girls, sex differences in performance were observed. Girls performed better than boys on an ostensibly feminine task, and boys did better when the same task was labeled masculine. Kobasigawa (1968) found that when female models applied a feminine label to feminine toys ("These toys are for girls. Girls like to play with these toys."), male subjects imitated the model less than when the toys were not explicitly labeled.

In sum, a variety of cues may be the starting point for observer inferences about model-observer similarity. The biological sex of the model is undoubtedly one such cue. The sex appropriateness of the behavior that the model exhibits may be another. Presumably, other sex-typed cues might be used as well. These might include the model's conformance to physical and personality norms for its sex (as perceived by the observer, of course), verbal labels applied to the behavior, or even the sex appropriateness of the clothes that the model wears. The observer's overall perception of the model's sex-role orientation and its match with the observer's own will ultimately determine whether the model is similar enough to the observer to act as an effective model.

A logical extension of this line of reasoning is that the preexisting attitudes and behaviors of audience members may also predict the effectiveness of nontraditional sex-role portrayals. Audience members who are already somewhat nontraditional in their sex-role preferences should learn more from nontraditional models than observers with traditional sex-role preferences. Perry and Perry (1975) verified that children with highly masculine sex-role preferences recalled more of a male model's behavior than a female model's, with the behaviors themselves neutral with respect to their sex appropriateness. However, the converse was not true for subjects with highly feminine sex-role preferences. Similarly, Stein et al. (1971) found that sex-role preference predicted performance on sex-typed tasks, although only among girls. These results imply that the sex-role preference of the observer may indeed help to explain the effectiveness of modeling sequences involving nontraditional sex-role behavior.

IMPLICATIONS FOR A CHANGE STRATEGY

It may be recalled that our practical motivation for reviewing literature on television and sex roles was to develop strategies for the development of television materials for the "Freestyle" project. Similar to the literature on sex-role stereotyping and its measurement, as discussed in Chapter 2, the literature on television and sex roles, as well as the additional materials on modeling, pointed to more cautions than strategies for combating stereotypes.

As reviewed in the present chapter, the content analytic and the correlational studies did not offer any significant insights regarding a change strategy. They only pointed out that typical television abounds with what adults would classify as sex-role stereotypes and that there are some correlations between viewership and children's attitudes. The correlations are not large, however, and the research designs too exploratory to yield useful conceptualizations. We found the experimental and the modeling studies (even though the latter seldom involved television) to be more useful to us. From them it was clear that characteristics of child viewers would have to be taken into account in researching the effects of counterstereotypic television materials, and such characteristics might well include sex-role attitudes as mediators. In communication terms, this meant that the audience for "Freestyle" should be segmented for research purposes. Yet, as discussed in Chapter 2, if such segmentation as well as measures of effects were to involve measures of sex-role stereotyping, there already existed pressing questions as to the validity of current measures.

Another implication of the experimental and modeling studies was that qualitative aspects of the television stimuli would probably be of great importance. Frequency of exposure to counterstereotypic materials might be important, but almost any experimental study purporting to affect children's sex-role attitudes has found interactions between characteristics of the stimuli and the child respondents. It seemed that at some point in the "Freestyle" project, we would have to come to grips with definitions of these characteristics—both as they applied to the children and to the television materials.

As will be seen in Chapters 4 through 7, we concentrated much of our original research on the replication and more detailed analysis of measures of children's sex-role stereotyping. We were not so much interested in finding the best possible measure—as many studies are now doing—as we were in gaining the ability to segment the child audience in ways meaningful for the development of counterstereotypic television materials. In Chapter 8, an initial study is reported of relationships between children's characteristics and some simplified characteristics of pilot materials from "Freestyle." Although we were never truly satisfied with our bases for audience segmentation, our experience in this area led us to suspect even more that the optimum change strategy would require as much or more effort in determining the qualities of television materials that would be most influential to the children. As it turned out, it was not so much a task of presenting counterstereotypic examples as of presenting ones with certain qualities. This made the research on modeling reviewed in the present chapter even more important to us than originally thought.

# 4

## SOME SIMPLE MEASURES OF CHILDREN'S STEREOTYPES

Prior to our original data gathering during the fall of 1977 on sex-role stereotypes, most research on this topic with children had involved using simple questionnaires or scaling attitudes about personality characteristics, activity preferences, or occupations. As discussed in Chapter 2, most such studies had focused upon male-female differences, as have the studies of television stereotypes described in Chapter 3.

As a part of the "Freestyle" project, our own initial research was motivated by several fundamental questions. One was whether these measures if applied to current-day children would yield the same results. Another question was the generality of results across the age range found in children from fourth- through sixth-grade classrooms. Finally, there was the question of the generality of results across the Anglo, Black, and Hispanic ethnic groups, which were to constitute the television audience.

The data gathered in these studies ultimately became the subject of more intensive analyses that led us to doubt the validity of simple measures of sex-role stereotyping and eventually to join other researchers in raising questions about studies that simply try to contrast male-female differences. The in-depth report of this study appears elsewhere (LaRose, Williams, Smith, Frost, & Eastman, 1978).

METHOD

Subjects

A total of 666 children participated in this and several of the subsequent studies. They included approximately equal representation of females and males, of Anglos, Blacks, and Hispanics, and of fourth, fifth, and sixth graders. Representing a variety of socio-economic backgrounds, the children came from a large California metropolitan area that included rural, suburban, and inner-city schools. Table 4.1 summarizes their characteristics.

Procedure

A female and male experimenter administered instruments to the children in their own classrooms. In schools with Hispanic students, a translator was available to help those needing assistance. All items were read aloud.

Instruments

Guttentag and Bray Semantic Differential Scales

The 12 bipolar items comprised adjectives referring to sex-typed characteristics of males and females in addition to two neutral-scale items. Each item contained a socially desirable pole and an undesirable pole, and the total instrument included five desirable and five undesirable characteristics for each sex. For example, one scale combined a socially desirable feminine-stereotyped characteristic ("gentle") with a socially undesirable masculine one ("rough"). Another combined a socially desirable masculine-stereotyped characteristic ("strong") with a negative feminine one ("weak"). These items were found by Guttentag and Bray (1976) to have practical utility in assessing children's sex-role-related stereotypes of "self" as well as the concepts of "most girls" ("girls should be") or "most boys" ("boys should be"). These have been recommended for use by children ranging from fourth to ninth grade.

The following adjectives were used in the present study, where M (male), F (female), and N (neutral) indicate the sex-type pole and the asterisk indicates social desirability. Certain items were slightly altered from the original to reduce the degree of abstractness or difficulty level for children.

| | |
|---|---|
| (M) Friendly* | - Shy |
| (F) Gentle* | - Rough |
| (F) Gives in* | - Stubborn |
| (M) Never cry* | - Cry a lot |
| (N) Troublemaker | - Obedient* |
| (F) Good looking* | - Ugly |

TABLE 4.1

Sample Characteristics

| Grade | Black | | Chicano | | Anglo | | Total | | Grade Total |
|---|---|---|---|---|---|---|---|---|---|
| | Boys | Girls | Boys | Girls | Boys | Girls | Boys | Girls | |
| Fourth | 35* | 29 | 17 | 14 | 43 | 36 | 95 | 80 | 175 |
| Fifth | 34 | 32 | 40 | 40 | 33 | 35 | 108 | 108 | 216 |
| Sixth | 50 | 40 | 30 | 29 | 34 | 28 | 121 | 97 | 218 |
| Total | 119 | 101 | 93 | 83 | 111 | 98 | 331 | 299 | — |
| Ethnic group total | 220 | | 176 | | 209 | | — | | 630 |

*Numbers do not add across and down since totals include 4 subjects classified as "other" ethnic origin and 21 students in an (ungraded) class of mentally gifted minors.

Note: Of the respondents, 36 had missing information for ethnic group status, grade, or sex.

41

| (N) | Loud | – Quiet* |
|---|---|---|
| (M) | Strong* | – Weak |
| (F) | Neat* | – Sloppy |
| (M) | Leader* | – Follower |
| (M) | Take chances* | – Careful |
| (M) | Worry about other people's feelings* | – Don't worry about other people's feelings |

In addition, anchors were added under each original scale segment, as in the following:

Gentle _____ Rough

| Very much | A little | I'm not sure | A little | Very much |
|---|---|---|---|---|

Each child rated the 12 items three times for "I am," "most girls," and "most boys."

## Activity Preferences

In order to assess children's liking for activities, 32 items were adapted from earlier work by Rosenberg and Sutton-Smith (1959, 1960) and from Holland's (1974) Social and Enterprising scales. These latter activities, which purport to predict occupational selection in adults, were chosen with the expectation that girls would show greater preference for Social scale items, while boys would prefer activities from the Enterprising scale. Subjects indicated on a Likert-type scale their amount of liking for each item from 1 (like very much) to 5 (dislike very much).

## Occupational Stereotypes

Based upon research by Iglitzin (1972) and Schlossberg and Goodman (1972), children rated 18 occupations regarding the ability of either women or men or girls or boys to perform each task. The items included 13 adult occupations and five child jobs; scale divisions ranged as follows: 1—only men; 2—mostly men; 3—both men and women; 4—mostly women; and 5—only women. Labels were changed to "boys" and "girls" for child job scales.

## RESULTS

### Guttentag and Bray Scales

#### Self-Ratings

In Figure 4.1, the means of girls' and boys' ratings of self are plotted to show differences in their self-concepts as measured by the scales. In general, ratings appear in the same area of the scale for both sexes, indicating that sex differences in ratings of self were not usually large. This was congruent with the work of Pedhazur and Tetenbaum (1979) and the Bem Sex Role Inventory. Yet differences were in the direction found earlier by Guttentag and Bray.

FIGURE 4.1

Children's Perceptions of Themselves

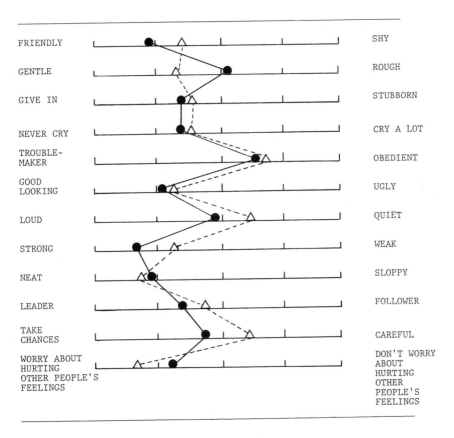

| FRIENDLY | | SHY |
| GENTLE | | ROUGH |
| GIVE IN | | STUBBORN |
| NEVER CRY | | CRY A LOT |
| TROUBLE-MAKER | | OBEDIENT |
| GOOD LOOKING | | UGLY |
| LOUD | | QUIET |
| STRONG | | WEAK |
| NEAT | | SLOPPY |
| LEADER | | FOLLOWER |
| TAKE CHANCES | | CAREFUL |
| WORRY ABOUT HURTING OTHER PEOPLE'S FEELINGS | | DON'T WORRY ABOUT HURTING OTHER PEOPLE'S FEELINGS |

△--△ Children's perceptions of Most Girls.
●—● Children's perceptions of Most Boys.

Source: Adapted from Guttentag and Bray (1976).

The inspection of the figures (not included here), which were broken down by grade and ethnicity, showed a very similar pattern to the results in Figure 4.1. In order to make a more general overall test of sex differences across grade and ethnic group, a composite score was calculated from those scales that a multiple discriminate analysis had shown most to contrast boys' as against girls' ratings. These scales were "friendly-shy," "gentle-rough," "strong-weak," and "take chances-careful." The higher the composite score, the more "female" the rating. The composite scores were then cast into a three-way analysis of variance with factors corresponding to sex-grade and ethnicity. As could be expected from the basis of the composite score, there were overall significant differences by sex, but there were none by grade or ethnicity. Of primary interest to us was the generality of sex differences within ethnic and grade subgroups. As shown in Table 4.2, with one minor exception the sex differences prevailed across all subdivisions of the sample.

TABLE 4.2

Sex, Grade, and Ethnic Differences in Composite
Personality Ratings of Self

| Ethnic Group | Boys' Ratings | Girls' Ratings |
|---|---|---|
| Black | | |
| Fourth grade | 2.4* | 3.1 |
| Fifth grade | 2.4* | 2.8 |
| Sixth grade | 2.3* | 2.9 |
| Hispanic | | |
| Fourth grade | 2.8 | 3.3 |
| Fifth grade | 2.5* | 3.0 |
| Sixth grade | 2.5* | 3.3 |
| Anglo | | |
| Fourth grade | 2.1* | 2.8 |
| Fifth grade | 2.1* | 2.9 |
| Sixth grade | 2.3* | 2.7 |

1 = male-like.
5 = female-like.
*Statistically significant differences between sexes ($p < .05$).
Note: Composite scores are averages across the scales "friendly-shy," "gentle-rough," "strong-weak," and "take chances-careful."

## Most Girls and Most Boys

Figure 4.2 shows the means for individual items on subjects' ratings of others, showing that differences in perceptions of the two stereotypes sometimes vary widely, and far more so than ratings of self. Stereotypes usually conformed to Guttentag and Bray's findings.

FIGURE 4.2

Children's Perceptions of Most Boys and Most Girls

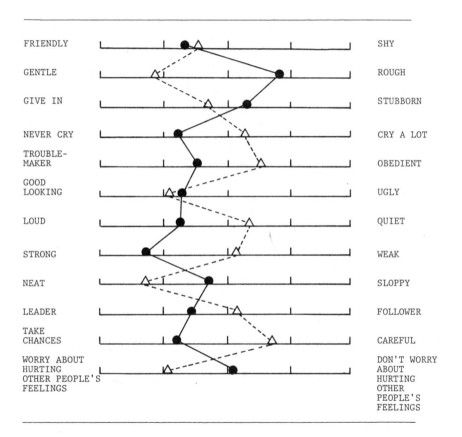

△ - - -△ Children's perceptions of Most Girls.
●———● Children's perceptions of Most Boys.

Source: Adapted from Guttentag and Bray (1976).

As with ratings of self, those four items best differentiating ratings of "most girls" from those of "most boys" were summed and a mean calculated for the sample broken down by sex, ethnic group, and grade (a higher mean indicates the tendency toward a feminine bias). The results in Table 4.3 for ratings of "most girls" indicate that with the exception of fifth-grade Anglos, boys tended to rate girls more stereotypically than the girls rated themselves. For ratings of "most boys" in Table 4.4, the opposite effect may be observed, although fewer mean differences reached significance between ratings by sex; girls in this instance rated boys more stereotypically than the boys themselves did.

TABLE 4.3

Sex, Grade, and Ethnic Differences in Composite
Personality of Most Girls

| Ethnic Group | Boys' Ratings | Girls' Ratings |
|---|---|---|
| Black | | |
| Fourth grade | 3.7* | 2.7 |
| Fifth grade | 3.5* | 2.4 |
| Sixth grade | 3.5* | 2.8 |
| Hispanic | | |
| Fourth grade | 3.2* | 2.5 |
| Fifth grade | 3.4* | 3.0 |
| Sixth grade | 3.3* | 2.6 |
| Anglo | | |
| Fourth grade | 3.7* | 2.7 |
| Fifth grade | 3.4 | 3.1 |
| Sixth grade | 3.6* | 3.0 |

1 = male-like.
5 = female-like.
*Statistically significant differences between sexes ($p < .05$).
Note: Scales summed were "strong-weak," "never cry-cry a lot," "worry-don't worry about hurting other people's feelings," and "friendly-shy."

TABLE 4.4

Sex, Grade, and Ethnic Differences in Composite
Personality Ratings of Most Boys

| Ethnic Group | Boys' Ratings | Girls' Ratings |
|---|---|---|
| Black | | |
| Fourth grade | 3.4* | 2.7 |
| Fifth grade | 3.0* | 2.6 |
| Sixth grade | 3.0* | 2.5 |
| Hispanic | | |
| Fourth grade | 3.0 | 2.9 |
| Fifth grade | 2.9* | 2.4 |
| Sixth grade | 3.0* | 2.3 |
| Anglo | | |
| Fourth grade | 3.0* | 2.2 |
| Fifth grade | 2.6 | 2.3 |
| Sixth grade | 2.3 | 2.3 |

1 = male-like.
5 = female-like.
*Statistically significant differences between sexes ($p < .05$).
Note: Scales summed were "trouble maker-obedient,"
"friendly-shy," "give in-stubborn," and "neat-sloppy."

Findings for ratings of others in large part supported those of
Guttentag and Bray (1977) in that subjects stereotyped the opposite
sex more than their own, stereotyped others more than themselves,
and in general followed stereotyped lines in their response patterns,
at least in their ratings of others. Our results reflect those of
studies with adults as well (Spence et al., 1974, 1975), as they suggest that ratings of self and others may represent entirely different
cognitive processes or that—less intriguing but equally problematic—
they may be the result of a socially desirable response bias. As
mentioned in Chapter 2, it may also be that children of this age
group have difficulty applying abstract concepts to themselves, while
they may rely on learned associations in rating others.

Activity Preferences

In Table 4.5, means are presented for the degree of liking of
particular activities by sex of the respondent. Multiple t tests

between means indicated that in general these activities showed the expected stereotyped liking patterns for boys and girls. A comparison of the results with those of Rosenberg and Sutton-Smith (1959, 1960) suggests little change in preferences over the years spanning the two studies.

TABLE 4.5

Liking for Play Activities by Sex

| Item | Boys | Girls |
|------|------|-------|
| Paper route | 2.4* | 3.2 |
| Cook | 2.6* | 1.3 |
| Race | 1.4 | 2.0* |
| Cops and robbers | 3.4 | 3.8* |
| Skateboarding | 1.4 | 1.7* |
| Football | 1.4 | 2.8* |
| Dress up | 4.4* | 2.9 |
| Basketball | 1.4 | 2.4* |
| Tools | 1.6 | 2.9* |
| Box | 2.0 | 3.6* |
| Sew | 4.0* | 1.6 |
| Baseball | 1.4 | 2.0* |
| Dolls | 4.7* | 3.0 |
| Swim | 1.2 | 1.2 |

1 = like very much.
5 = dislike very much.
*Denotes significant mean difference between the sexes
($p < .01$).

Table 4.6 presents selected ethnic differences and similarities in activity liking, and Table 4.7 contains the three most often mentioned favorite activities by sex and ethnic group. Contrary to prior research, girls of all grades and ethnic groups expressed high favoritism for vigorous outdoor sports. Boys' responses followed traditional lines.

The selection of items from Holland's (1974) Social and Enterprising scales allowed the examination of items that could be expected to show differences in girls' and boys' responses. The Social scale is related to service occupations traditionally labeled as

## TABLE 4.6

### Activity Preferences by Sex and Ethnic Group

|  | Boys' Activity | Girls' Activity |
|---|:---:|:---:|
| **Activity not influenced by ethnic group** | | |
| With boy-girl differences[a] | | |
| Have a paper route | + | − |
| Play football* | + | − |
| Use tools* | + | − |
| Box* | + | − |
| Build rocket models | + | − |
| Play basketball* | + | − |
| Play baseball* | + | − |
| Cook* | − | + |
| Dress up* | − | + |
| Sew* | − | + |
| Play with dolls* | − | + |
| Dance | − | + |
| Take care of children | − | + |
| Without boy-girl differences | | |
| Go skateboarding | + | + |
| Go swimming* | + | + |
| Belong to social clubs | + | + |
| Go to parties | + | + |
| Make new friends | + | + |
| Sell something | + | + |
| Talk about current events | + | + |
| Run own business | + | + |
| Give talks | + | + |

(continued)

Table 4.6, continued

| | Boys' Activity | Girls' Activity |
|---|---|---|
| Be president of a club | + | + |
| Meet important people | + | + |
| Lead others in reaching a goal | + | + |
| Get others to do what you want | + | + |
| Watch television after dinner | + | + |
| Read comics | + | + |
| **Activity with boy-girl differences by ethnic group[a]** | | |
| Black | | |
| Go to sports events | + | – |
| Play baseball* | + | – |
| Race* | + | – |
| Play cops and robbers* | + | – |
| Hispanic | | |
| Go to sports events | + | – |
| Play baseball* | + | – |
| Play cops and robbers* | + | – |
| Write letters | – | + |
| Help others | – | + |
| Go to meetings | – | + |
| Anglo | | |
| Race* | + | – |
| Write letters | – | + |
| Go to religious services | – | + |
| Help someone get elected | – | + |

+ = shows greater preference for the activity.
– = shows less preference for the activity.
*Denotes activities used in Rosenberg and Sutton-Smith's original (1959, 1960) studies.
[a]$p < .05$

feminine, such as a nurse or elementary school teacher, while the Enterprising scale relates to sales and entrepreneurship, which have typically belonged to the realm of the male. Findings as shown in Table 4.8 indicate (congruent with Holland's results on an older sample) that more differences occur between girls and boys on the Social scale than on the Enterprising scale.

TABLE 4.7

Sex, Grade, and Ethnic Differences in Children's
Favorite Play Activities

|  | Boys' Ratings | Girls' Ratings |
|---|---|---|
| Ethnic group |  |  |
| Black | Football* | Baseball |
|  | Basketball | Kickball |
|  | Baseball | House |
| Hispanic | Football | Soccer |
|  | Baseball | Handball |
|  | Basketball | Pins/baseball |
| Anglo | Baseball | Football/baseball |
|  | Football | Soccer |
|  | Soccer | Kickball |
| Grade |  |  |
| Fourth | Football | Handball |
|  | Baseball | Kickball |
|  | Soccer | Baseball |
| Fifth | Baseball | Soccer |
|  | Football | Baseball |
|  | Basketball | Handball |
| Sixth | Football | Baseball |
|  | Baseball | Soccer |
|  | Soccer | Kickball |

*The three most frequently occurring responses to the open-ended question, "What do you like to play the most?" All choices are listed where ties occurred.

TABLE 4.8

Liking for Enterprising and Social Activities by Sex

| Item | Boys' Ratings | Girls' Ratings |
|---|---|---|
| Write letters (S) | 2.5* | 1.6 |
| Go to religious services (S) | 2.2* | 1.9 |
| Belong to social clubs (S) | 2.3 | 2.2 |
| Help others with their problems (S) | 1.8* | 1.6 |
| Take care of children (S) | 2.4* | 1.5 |
| Go to parties (S) | 1.4* | 1.2 |
| Dance (S) | 2.6* | 1.6 |
| Go to meetings (S, E) | 2.8 | 2.5 |
| Go to sports events (S) | 1.2 | 2.0* |
| Make new friends (S) | 1.4* | 1.3 |
| Get others to do what you want them to do (E) | 2.9 | 3.2 |
| Sell things (E) | 2.1 | 2.2 |
| Talk about current events (E) | 2.2 | 2.3 |
| Run own business (E) | 1.6 | 2.0* |
| Give talks (E) | 3.0 | 2.8 |
| Be president of a club (E) | 1.7 | 1.8 |
| Supervise others (E) | 2.1 | 2.0 |
| Meet important people (E) | 1.4* | 1.2 |
| Lead a group to reach a goal (E) | 1.8 | 1.9 |
| Help someone get elected (E) | 1.8* | 1.7 |

E = Enterprising.
S = Social.
1 = like very much.
5 = dislike very much.
*Denotes a significant mean difference between the sexes
($p < .01$).

In order to make male–female comparisons across sample subgroups of grade and ethnic groups, a score was calculated for each child that reflected the number of social activities (out of 10) and the number of enterprising activities (out of 11) that had been rated on the "liking" side of the original scale. These results are summarized in Tables 4.9 and 4.10, respectively.

TABLE 4.9

Scores on Social Activities Scale by Sex, Grade, and Ethnic Group

| Ethnic Group | Boys' Ratings | Girls' Ratings |
|---|---|---|
| Black | | |
| Fourth grade | 8.5 | 8.6 |
| Fifth grade | 8.4* | 9.4 |
| Sixth grade | 7.9 | 8.3 |
| Hispanic | | |
| Fourth grade | 7.5 | 8.1 |
| Fifth grade | 7.3* | 8.0 |
| Sixth grade | 6.7* | 8.6 |
| Anglo | | |
| Fourth grade | 7.0 | 7.2 |
| Fifth grade | 6.1* | 7.4 |
| Sixth grade | 7.2 | 7.9 |
| Holland's (1974) original | | |
| college sample | 5.9 | 7.7 |

*Indicates statistical significance between means for boys and girls ($p < .05$).

Note: Data are based on the number of activities liked out of 10.

TABLE 4.10

Scores on Enterprising Activities Scale by Sex, Grade, and Ethnic Group

| Ethnic Group | Boys' Ratings | Girls' Ratings |
|---|---|---|
| Black | | |
| Fourth grade | 8.4 | 8.3 |
| Fifth grade | 8.2 | 8.6 |
| Sixth grade | 8.2 | 7.5 |
| Hispanic | | |
| Fourth grade | 6.4* | 8.6 |
| Fifth grade | 7.3 | 6.6 |
| Sixth grade | 6.4 | 7.6 |
| Anglo | | |
| Fourth grade | 8.0* | 7.1 |
| Fifth grade | 6.7 | 6.8 |
| Sixth grade | 7.2 | 7.5 |
| Holland's (1974) original | | |
| college sample | 6.2 | 6.2 |

*Indicates statistical significance between means for boys and girls ($p < .05$).

Note: Data are based on the number of activities liked out of 11.

Again, only the choices of social activities (Table 4.9) most consistently differentiate the children by sex in the various ethnic and grade subgroups. Only in two instances did a statistically significant contrast appear for choices of enterprising activities (Table 4.10). Examining age trends, younger children were least differentiated by sex in their ratings of social activities.

TABLE 4.11

Children's Perceptions of the Sex Distribution
of Occupations

| | Boys' Ratings | Girls' Ratings |
|---|---|---|
| Adult occupation | | |
| Truck driver | 2.1 | 2.5* |
| Doctor | 2.6 | 2.8* |
| Secretary | 3.9 | 3.8 |
| Elementary school teacher | 3.0 | 3.1 |
| Auto mechanic | 1.6 | 2.0* |
| Police officer | 2.4 | 2.7* |
| Architect | 2.2 | 2.4* |
| Business executive | 2.4 | 2.6* |
| Taxi driver | 2.2 | 2.2 |
| Nurse | 4.2 | 4.1 |
| Plumber | 1.8 | 1.9 |
| Mayor | 2.2 | 2.4* |
| Housekeeper | 4.0 | 4.0 |
| | | |
| Children's job | | |
| Pack groceries | 2.6 | 2.9* |
| Babysitter | 3.8 | 3.9 |
| Wash cars | 2.2 | 2.5* |
| Mow lawns | 1.9 | 2.3* |
| Run a lemonade stand | 2.8 | 3.2* |

1 = only for men.
5 = only for women.
*Denotes significant mean difference between sexes ($p < .01$).

Occupational Stereotypes

Children's ratings of the ability of males and females to perform certain jobs generally followed stereotyped lines. As shown in Table 4.11, men are perceived as able to drive trucks and women as able to serve as nurses. The small number of jobs stereotypically female reflects their traditional range of choices in the job market. Boys and girls tended to restrict these female jobs to women, with no significant differences in ratings. For occupations traditionally male, however, a different pattern emerges. Girls showed a greater tendency to respond that women could perform these tasks, while boys tended to exclude women. The only exceptions were the very highly stereotyped male occupations of taxi driver and plumber. Results were similar for the child jobs, and further analysis indicated that children who tended to stereotype adult occupations also tended to stereotype child jobs. There were no major contrasts by ethnic or grade subgroups on male-female differentiation.

SUMMARY

The initial aim in this original research was to determine if similar results would be obtained from current-day children in response to measures presumed to gauge the stereotyping of personality, activities, and occupations. Generally, the present results in terms of simple tabulation types of analyses were similar to earlier studies. Another aim was to assess sex differences within ethnic and grade-level subgroups. With only a few exceptions, boy and girl differences in these general measures of stereotyping prevailed in subgroupings of the sample.

Our analyses of these data, however, did not stop on the level of simple tabulations. We were interested in the psychometric properties of the measures and, particularly, in relations across domains of stereotyping. The more major analyses next undertaken are reported in the following chapters.

# 5

## COMPLEX PROBLEMS WITH
## SIMPLE MEASURES

There were both practical and theoretical reasons for further analyses of the sex-role stereotype scales reported by Guttentag and Bray (1976, 1977). On the practical side was that the "Freestyle" project, like Guttentag and Bray's school project, was to counter sex-role stereotyping by the use of intervention materials. Although researchers such as Bem (1974) had already raised issue with bipolar male-female comparisons, there was a practical utility in using scales for which there was a prior body of data from a project with children. But there remained questions of the reliability and validity of the Guttentag and Bray scales, questions not addressed in their reports.

On the theoretical side were questions of what type of mediational model of sex-role judgments might be derived from analyses of children's use of the scales. Presumably, if sex-role stereotyping were a fundamental mediator, we would expect factor analyses of the scale intercorrelations to yield evidence that the underlying use of the 12 or so scales was a basic judgmental dimension of male versus female. The finding of a single major bipolar factor would be evidence that children were indeed judging sex-role concepts on a single continuum. By contrast, two major factors each clustering scales associated with the different sexes and perhaps biased by social desirability would be evidence that judgments were more independent for each sex. Additionally, there was the question of the factor similarity of judgments of self as well as others of the same or opposite sex.

In this chapter we report two stages of further analyses of our data gathered with the Guttentag and Bray scales from the sample of 666 children described in Chapter 4. The first stage was a reliability analysis; the second, the factor analytic applications.

RELIABILITY

Reliability estimates (alpha) (Cronbach, 1951) were calculated for the female socially desirable scale items, for the corresponding male items, and for these two sets combined with the two neutral items for a total scale estimate. Such estimates were calculated separately for boy and girl respondents and for the three concepts.

As can be seen in Table 5.1, it is clear from the alpha estimates that the Guttentag and Bray scales are not particularly reliable, whether they are calculated on the male items, the female items, or the total set of 12 ratings. However, in examining the reliability measures, two factors should be considered: alpha would undoubtedly be increased through the addition of items, and alpha is generally considered a lower-bound internal consistency reliability estimate (Cronbach, 1951).

TABLE 5.1

Guttentag and Bray Semantic Differential Test: Internal
Consistency Reliability (alpha) for Ratings of "Self,"
"Most Boys," and "Most Girls" by Sex of
Respondent and Total Sample

| Rating Category | Scale | Respondents | | |
| | | Girls (n = 313) | Boys (n = 350) | Total Sample (n = 663) |
|---|---|---|---|---|
| Self | Female | .40 | .43 | .42 |
| | Male | .20 | .33 | .38 |
| | Total | .44 | .41 | .45 |
| Most girls | Female | .44 | .65 | .63 |
| | Male | .37 | .55 | .57 |
| | Total | .44 | .68 | .69 |
| Most boys | Female | .64 | .60 | .68 |
| | Male | .33 | .43 | .40 |
| | Total | .61 | .58 | .66 |

Note: Under each rating category, the female scale consists of five socially desirable personality characteristics stereotypical of females; the male scale contains five such items for males; the total scale contains the male and female scales plus two neutral items.

The reliability data do tend to reflect group characteristics often found in ratings of sex-role stereotypes (Rosenkrantz et al., 1968). Children tend to stereotype concepts of other girls and boys to a greater degree than themselves, and this appears to be reflected in larger reliability estimates for these former concepts. Also, children tend to stereotype the opposite sex more than they stereotype themselves in terms of these generalized concepts, and this is reflected in the present results. However, to reiterate cautions that we have expressed previously, we cannot conclude from the data that children "stereotype" themselves at all. In the present case, it would appear that perhaps in the absence of specific personal experience, stereotypes may be reflected in the children's ratings with a correspondent increase in reliability (for example, girls' ratings of "most boys"). However, when firsthand knowledge is available, as in self-ratings or ratings of others of the same sex, the children may have found the task more difficult, and we have evidence of other processes at work, the nature of which we have speculated upon elseshere.

Practically speaking, however, the low reliability estimates raise serious questions regarding the utility of these scales—for example, in the diagnosis of sex-role stereotyping in groups of children or in the assessment of the effects of intervention programs.

## FACTOR STRUCTURE

In the second stage of the analyses, the question was raised whether, despite modest reliability, factor analysis would yield interpretable dimensions of judgment. Former studies using factor analysis on this type of data have not evaluated possible interactions among sex of respondent, concepts being rated (for example, "self"), and the individual scale items. Thus, for one thing, factor analyses were undertaken separately for the data obtained from boys and girls. Further, the variables in each analysis were concept-by-scale item combinations—for example, "self: strong-weak" or "most girls: neat-sloppy." Principal components analyses were employed, and the factor structures subjected to varimax rotation.

Tables 5.2 and 5.3 summarize the results of the two factor analyses for boys and girls, respectively. Of initial consequence in these results was that neither boys nor girls tended to rate the concepts on any global factors. Instead, dimensions of judgment tended to be reflected in a variety of item-specific factors, with definite interaction with the concepts rated. Moreover, the judgmental dimensions were apparently different for boy and girl raters, a finding consistent with that of Pedhazur and Tetenbaum (1979), who found

with the Bem Sex Role Inventory different factor patterns for males
and females.

It has already been argued by others (Chapter 2) that boys and
girls do not tend to evaluate the present concepts in terms of male-
versus-female judgments, and this was reflected in the present results, even though the Guttentag and Bray items contain adjectival
opposites that encourage such bipolar judgments. It can also be
noted that the children's use of scale items did not tend to cluster
into judgmental dimensions reflecting social desirability, nor were
the scale items subsumed by the concepts rated.

In addition to a number of particularistic dimensions, boys
tended to reflect two general dimensions that apparently represent
an impression of girls as "obedient, quiet, and cautious" as well as
"friendly, cry a lot, good looking, and weak." Both factors mix
social desirability. Boys' relatively major dimensions for evaluating themselves as well as for the concept of "most boys" were along
the lines of "good looking and strong." The remaining dimensions
used in boys' judgments tended to reflect individual scale items,
either as associated with "self," "most boys," or the combination
of these two concepts, thus indicating a relatively complex and multifaceted judgmental scheme as against a global male-female or socially desirable framework.

The results of the factor analysis of the girls' ratings also
reflected a variety of dimensions, which again mixed combinations
of social desirability, individual scale items, and concepts. The
only item combinations relative to "self" or "most girls" were "good-
looking" and "strong" dimensions and "quiet, cautious" dimensions.
Girls tended to rate boys primarily on a "rough" dimension. They
also related the ratings of "never cry" and "strong" with the concept "most boys." Most ratings, again, reflected a multifaceted
evaluation scheme.

It may be that certain items were so low on reliability that
they tended to be omitted from the factor structures, such as "gives
in-stubborn" for boys or "neat-sloppy" for girls.

In all, the interpretation of the results of these analyses is
considerably different from assumptions underlying practical applications of these scales. Previously, all items were used to compare boys' and girls' ratings of themselves and others, or the scales
were used to index changes resulting from intervention programs.
Beyond the problems of reliability, it is clear that boys and girls
attach different emphasis upon which scale items they use for concepts. Thus a straightforward comparison of boys' and girls' ratings
on any other dimensions than those that appeared in both analyses may
be based upon a false assumption of comparability. That is to say,
some scales are more relevant to girls than to boys and differentially
relevant for each in terms of the concepts to which they are applied.

## TABLE 5.2

Boys: Factors in the Use of Guttentag and Bray
Semantic Differential Test Items

| Factor | Factor Label | Scale | Percentage of Variance | Factor Loading | Mean |
|---|---|---|---|---|---|
| I | Girls | Obedient-troublemaker (girls) | 22.2 | .59 | 3.4 |
| | | Quiet-loud (girls) | | .66 | 3.1 |
| | | Take chances-cautious (girls) | | -.50 | 2.2 |
| II | Self/boys | Good looking-ugly (self) | 17.4 | .75 | 4.0 |
| | | Good looking-ugly (boys) | | .59 | 4.0 |
| | | Strong-weak (self) | | .54 | 4.3 |
| III | Girls | Friendly-shy (girls) | 15.5 | .56 | 3.1 |
| | | Never cry-cry a lot (girls) | | .54 | 2.3 |
| | | Strong-weak (girls) | | .66 | 2.2 |
| IV | Self/boys | Take chances-cautious (self) | 9.3 | .67 | 3.2 |
| | | Take chances-cautious (boys) | | .67 | 3.5 |
| V | Self/boys | Never cry-cry a lot (self) | 8.0 | .56 | 3.7 |
| | | Never cry-cry a lot (boys) | | .71 | 3.9 |

| | | | | | |
|---|---|---|---|---|---|
| VI | Boys | Quiet-loud (boys) | 5.5 | .65 | 2.6 |
| VII | Self | Obedient-troublemaker (self) | 4.7 | .70 | 3.6 |
| VIII | Boys | Neat-sloppy (self) | | .60 | 4.1 |
| | | Neat-sloppy (boys) | 4.3 | .71 | 3.7 |
| IX | Boys | Friendly-shy (boys) | 3.8 | .64 | 4.0 |
| X | Self/boys | Worry about hurting other people's feelings–don't worry about hurting other people's feelings (self) | | .52 | 4.2 |
| | | Worry about hurting other people's feelings–don't worry about hurting other people's feelings (boys) | 3.6 | .57 | 4.3 |
| XI | Self | Quiet-loud (self) | 2.9 | .62 | 3.0 |
| XII | Self | Gentle-rough (self) | 2.7 | .65 | 3.0 |

Note: Factor loadings > .50.

61

TABLE 5.3

Girls: Factors in the Use of Guttentag and Bray
Semantic Differential Test Items

| Factor | Factor Label | Scale | Percentage of Variance | Factor Loading | Mean |
|---|---|---|---|---|---|
| I | Boys | Gentle–rough (boys) | 21.1 | .78 | 1.8 |
| II | Self/girls | Good looking–ugly (self) | 16.2 | .53 | 3.7 |
| | | Good looking–ugly (girls) | | .51 | 4.2 |
| | | Strong–weak (girls) | | .62 | 3.6 |
| III | Girls | Quiet–loud (girls) | 10.7 | .70 | 3.6 |
| | | Take chances–cautious (girls) | | -.54 | 2.3 |
| IV | Self/girls | Worry about hurting other people's feelings–don't worry about hurting other people's feelings (self) | 9.4 | .92 | 4.1 |
| | | Worry about hurting other people's feelings–don't worry about hurting other people's feelings (girls) | | .59 | 4.1 |

| | | | | |
|---|---|---|---|---|
| V | Self/girls | Leader–follower (self) | 8.1 | .57 | 3.2 |
| | | Leader–follower (girls) | | .85 | 3.2 |
| VI | Self | Obedient–troublemaker (self) | 6.1 | .56 | 3.8 |
| VII | Girls | Gives in–stubborn (girls) | 5.6 | .83 | 3.6 |
| VIII | Boys | Never cry–cry a lot (boys) | 4.9 | .56 | 3.7 |
| | | Strong–weak (boys) | | .60 | 4.0 |
| IX | Boys | Obedient–troublemaker (boys) | 4.2 | .60 | 2.1 |
| X | Boys | Friendly–shy (boys) | 4.0 | .45 | 3.3 |
| XI | Self/boys | Gentle–rough (self) | 3.7 | .60 | 3.6 |
| | | Gentle–rough (girls) | | .52 | 4.2 |
| XII | Girls | Never cry–cry a lot (girls) | 3.2 | .66 | 3.3 |

Note: Factor loadings > .50.

63

Furthermore, results also appear relevant to issues raised in Chapter 2 regarding the development of scales to measure sex-role stereotyping and psychological sex. Unfortunately, Guttentag and Bray do not report the manner of their scales' derivation, but one may suspect that items comprise what adults conceive as constituting sex-role stereotypes for females and males. A second point regards the actual ratings: Do they reflect social desirability, self-esteem, or sex-role bias? All three? Or something else? The extrication of underlying sex-role factors is difficult, particularly as the scale construction tends to maximize the effects of social desirability in the children's ratings. As mentioned in Chapter 4, self-ratings on the scales were not always highly differentiated in girls' and boys' responses, adding credence to the suggestion that social desirability, and not just sex-role bias, may represent one mediator underlying the ratings. A fourth consideration may not fit the concepts as they are actually rated. A clue to this difficulty comes from the work of Spence and her colleagues (Spence et al., 1974, 1975; Spence & Helmreich, 1978) who discovered that some sex-typed attributes are best conceived as unipolar; others, as bipolar.

## IMPLICATIONS

The main admonition from these analyses was that the Guttentag and Bray scales, although best known for use with this age group, could be used further only with great caution. Optimally, if personality ratings are desired, one should develop an entirely new instrument. On the other hand, personality characteristics were only one domain of concepts that we explored for evidence of stereotyping by children. Hence, rather than pursue the development of a new instrument, we focused our further work on other concept domains, making only selected use of our data from the Guttentag and Bray scales for comparative purposes.

# 6
## ARE ACTIVITY INTERESTS AND PERSONALITY STEREOTYPING RELATED?

The majority of studies concerning sex-role stereotyping in children have dealt with a single concept domain, such as sex-typed personality characteristics (Guttentag & Bray, 1977; Williams et al., 1975), activity preferences (Rosenberg & Sutton-Smith, 1959, 1960), or sex-related occupational stereotypes (Garrett et al., 1977; Schlossberg & Goodman, 1972). At the time of our research, we knew of no published effort to assess the generality of children's stereotype biases across concept domains, especially those with implications concerning the socialization of sex-role attitudes. Bem's work with adults (Bem & Lenney, 1976) suggested that such relationships may exist, although not in a consistent manner. Children's activity preferences are concrete, everyday choices for them.

In the rationale underlying the "Freestyle" media project, it was reasoned that preadolescent children's sex-role biases could limit their activity choices and hence the opportunity to develop along lines that could lead to certain occupations. For example, a young girl might avoid model building as a "boys' thing" and thus never develop skills that might be useful for occupations requiring craftmanship, fabrication, or perhaps engineering. More theoretically, there was the question of sex-role bias as a fundamental mediator in behavior. The more fundamental it was, then, the more certain sex-role biases would affect different domains of a child's attitudes, choices, and behavior.

The present project was a straightforward attempt to assess relationships between children's responses to personality rating instruments and scales of activity preferences. The data were so selected as to maximize chances of revealing relationships between these types of judgments, if such relationships did exist. The analytic model was canonical correlation.

METHOD

A description of the subjects and the data-gathering procedure appears in Chapter 4. Activity preferences were those taken from Rosenberg and Sutton-Smith (1959, 1960) and Holland's (1974) Social and Enterprising scales, also described in Chapter 4. Personality adjectives were selected from Guttentag and Bray's instrument (1977), with consideration of our findings presented in Chapters 4 and 5.

As the purpose of the present study was to examine the relationships between two types of measures of sex-role stereotypes, only those activity preferences were used that differentiated significantly between boys and girls in a $t$ test between means ($p < .05$). All such significant differences by sex were congruent with previous findings on stereotypes of activity preferences (Holland, 1974; Rosenberg & Sutton-Smith, 1959, 1960). The internal consistency (alpha) (Cronbach, 1951) on activity items was estimated at .78.

The main analyses were canonical correlations of activity sets with personality ratings representing psychological sex separately for girl and boy raters. Although we knew that the reliability of this instrument was low, we were now interested in correlations between individual personality scales and activity ratings.

RESULTS

Tables 6.1 and 6.2 summarize the results of the canonical correlation analyses for girls and boys, respectively.

The most general interpretation was that moderate degrees of relation were found between selected activity preferences and personality self-ratings in both analyses of boys' and girls' data. Two variates were extracted in each analysis, and the canonical correlation coefficients ranged from a low of .50 to a high of .56, all significant at the $p < .01$ level. Yet beyond this, an inspection of the clusters of individual scales did not reveal any consistent patterns. Thus, for example, neither analysis revealed a tendency for either male- or female-stereotyped activities to dominate in a pattern of results. The results seemed more tied to particular scale relations between personality and activity ratings. Boys, for example, showed a relation (Variate I) between "helping others with their problems" and "worrying about others' feelings," rating the latter more neutral than as a strictly feminine-stereotyped personality characteristic. On Variate II, "playing football, using tools, and boxing" were related to the bias of giving a high male rating to the personality characteristic "strong." Or for girls, "sewing" and "helping others with their problems" were related to ratings on the "cautious-take chances"

# TABLE 6.1

Male Subjects: Canonical Variates of Relations of Personality Characteristics and Activity Preferences

## Activity Preference[a]

| | Variate I (Rc = .55) | | | Variate II (Rc = .50) | |
|---|---|---|---|---|---|
| Loading | Sex-Role Preference[b] | Scale Mean | Sex-Role Preference[b] | Loading | Scale Mean |
| .16 | (M) Race | 1.4 | (F) Cook | -.23 | 2.6 |
| -.27 | (M) Skateboard | 1.4 | (M) Play football | .36 | 1.5 |
| .33 | (M) Use tools to fix a bike | 1.6 | (M) Use tools to fix a bike | .33 | 1.6 |
| -.35 | (M) Box | 2.0 | (M) Box | .23 | 2.0 |
| .21 | (F) Go to religious services | 2.2 | (F) Play with dolls | -.17 | 4.7 |
| .45 | (F) Help others with their problems | 1.8 | (F) Go to religious services | -.18 | 2.2 |
| .30 | (F) Take care of children | 2.4 | (F) Dance | .24 | 2.6 |
| -.35 | (M) Get others to do what you want | 2.9 | (F) Go to meetings | .24 | 2.8 |
| -.15 | (F) Play with dolls | 4.7 | (M) Get others to do what you want | .20 | 2.9 |
| | | | (M) Meet important people | .27 | 1.5 |

## Personality Characteristic Stereotype[c]

| Loading | Female | Male | Scale Mean | Female | Male | Loading | Scale Mean |
|---|---|---|---|---|---|---|---|
| .34 | Gentle | Rough | 3.0 | Shy | Friendly | .15 | 4.0 |
| .17 | Good looking | Ugly | 2.0 | Gentle | Rough | -.31 | 3.0 |
| .22 | Quiet | Loud | 3.0 | Good looking | Ugly | .19 | 2.0 |
| .20 | Neat | Sloppy | 1.9 | Weak | Strong | -.62 | 4.3 |
| .74 | Worry about hurting others' feelings-Don't worry about hurting others' feelings | | 2.2 | Neat | Sloppy | .32 | 2.0 |
| | | | | Follower | Leader | -.22 | 3.5 |

[a] Activity preferences are scored from 1 to 5: 1 = like very much; 5 = dislike very much.
[b] (M) = Male preferred; (F) = Female preferred.
[c] Personality characteristics are scored from 1 to 5: 1 = female stereotypes; 5 = male stereotypes.
Female stereotypes are listed to the left of the hyphen.

## TABLE 6.2

Female Subjects: Canonical Variates of Relations of Personality Characteristics and Activity Preferences

### Activity Preference[a]

| | Variate I (Rc = .56) | | | Variate II (Rc = .53) | |
|---|---|---|---|---|---|
| Loading | Sex-Role Preference[b] | Scale Mean | Loading | Sex-Role Preference[b] | Scale Mean |
| -.23 | (M) Race | 2.1 | .39 | (F) Cook | 1.3 |
| .39 | (M) Use tools to fix a bike | 2.9 | -.22 | (M) Play football | 2.9 |
| .38 | (M) Box | 3.6 | .45 | (F) Play dress up | 2.9 |
| -.43 | (F) Sew | 1.7 | .56 | (M) Play baseball | 2.0 |
| -.33 | (M) Play baseball | 2.0 | -.16 | (F) Help others with their problems | 1.6 |
| -.41 | (F) Help others with their problems | 1.6 | .22 | (F) Dance | 1.6 |
| .21 | (M) Go to sports events | 2.0 | .24 | (F) Go to meetings | 2.5 |
| .23 | (F) Make new friends | 1.3 | -.19 | (F) Make new friends | 1.3 |
| -.21 | (M) Build rocket models | 3.6 | -.25 | (M) Build rocket models | 3.6 |
| | | | .24 | (M) Meet important people | 1.3 |

### Personality Characteristic Stereotype[c]

| | Variate I | | | | Variate II | | |
|---|---|---|---|---|---|---|---|
| Loading | Female | Male | Scale Mean | Loading | Female | Male | Scale Mean |
| -.29 | Gentle | Rough | 2.4 | .26 | Gentle | Rough | 2.4 |
| -.31 | Obedient | Troublemaker | 2.2 | .44 | Give in | Never give in | 3.4 |
| -.19 | Good looking | Ugly | 2.3 | .52 | Good looking | Ugly | 2.3 |
| -.22 | Quiet | Loud | 2.7 | .48 | Neat | Sloppy | 1.8 |
| -.32 | Weak | Strong | 3.8 | -.30 | Follower | Leader | 3.2 |
| -.38 | Neat | Sloppy | 1.8 | | | | |
| -.17 | Follower | Leader | 3.2 | | | | |
| -.51 | Cautious | Take chances | 2.5 | | | | |

[a] Activity preferences are scored from 1 to 5: 1 = like very much; 5 = dislike very much.
[b] (M) = Male preferred; (F) = Female preferred.
[c] Personality characteristics are scored from 1 to 5: 1 = female stereotype; 5 = male stereotype. Female stereotypes are listed to the left of the hyphen.

personality scale (Variate I), although their mean ratings on the latter were in the neutral zone of the scale. There was even evidence of counterstereotypical relations in the girls' second variate—"playing baseball" was related to personality ratings of "good looking-ugly" and "give in-never give in," and the mean on the latter scale was male biased.

## DISCUSSION

Despite the sex-role bias in selecting personality and activity measures, the present study did not reveal a fundamental sex-stereotyped dimension underlying both sets of variables or their overall relation. If sex-role bias were a highly salient mediator in children's perceptions, it would be expected that personality characteristics stereotyped for one sex would predict activity interests preferred by that sex.

Factors underlying these findings may represent multiple basis. For example, the low reliability of the Guttentag and Bray scales may account for the lack of precision in individual items, or children may not hold well-defined concepts in these areas. The abstract nature of adjectives in the latter domain may be a factor, or ratings may be based primarily on a socially desirable response set.

On the other hand, perhaps we should not expect biases in personality attitudes to influence so directly attitudes about engaging in activities. The exception might be where the activity and the personality characteristic have some common quality, such as in several of the individual personality-activity scale relations just discussed.

The results of this analysis, along with the lack of finding basic sex-role stereotyping factors in the Guttentag and Bray scale data (Chapter 5), added to our doubts that sex-role bias in children, or perhaps in general, was the fundamental or global concept that much earlier literature would lead one to believe.

# 7

## ARE OCCUPATIONAL STEREOTYPES RELATED TO ACTIVITY AND PERSONALITY STEREOTYPES?

Even more practically related to the "Freestyle" project was the question of whether judgments of which sex could fill selected adult occupations would be related to a child's other stereotyped responses—in this case, personality ratings of self and others—as well as activity preference ratings. In essence, this was the third study in which we sought evidence of sex-role bias as a fundamental mediator. This interest was parallel to the intervention strategy of Guttentag and Bray (1976) when they developed "nonsexist" curriculum materials for here-and-now concepts on the assumption that this would have effects on reducing sex-role stereotyping as a part of the socialization process. Even more directly related to "Freestyle" research was the report by Leifer and Lesser (1976) who suggested that attacking a child's immediate stereotypes was a basis for alleviating later biases in career choice.

Our analytic model differed from the prior (Chapter 6) canonical model in several ways. First, since we were focusing upon stereotypes of "others" in occupations, we included not only personality ratings of self in this study but also children's ratings of "most boys" and "most girls." Second, in order to simplify the analyses, occupational ratings were reduced to one female and two male categories of occupations. And third, to study the relative contribution of personality and activity stereotyping to occupational stereotyping, a multiple correlation model was employed.

## METHOD

Subjects and data gathering are described in Chapter 4. In the current analysis, the Guttentag and Bray scale scoring was transformed such that maximum female-stereotyped responses were scored 1 and maximum male, 5. The scales were repeated for the concepts "I am," "most boys are," and "most girls are."

Activity preference items were taken from research by Rosenberg and Sutton-Smith (1959, 1960) and Holland (1974). Then, 26 items that in pilot testing had discriminated (t test; $p < .05$) between girls' and boys' preferences were selected for use here. The item format consisted of a Likert-type, 5-step rating scale from 1 (like very much) to 5 (dislike very much).

Based on the research of Schlossberg and Goodman (1972) and Iglitzin (1972), 18 adult occupations were initially selected for the occupational stereotype measures. Responses to the question, "Who can do this job?" were made on the 5-step scale: (1) only women, (2) mostly women, (3) both men and women, (4) mostly men, and (5) only men.

Estimates of reliability (alpha) (Cronbach, 1951) were calculated on each set of scales, as insufficient information was available from previous studies. Again, the Guttentag and Bray scales' estimated internal consistency for self-ascribed personality characteristics was .45; for ratings of personality characteristics of "most girls," .69; and for "most boys," .66. Although the first represented a low reliability, it was felt that the exploratory nature of the study could justify cautious use of the ratings. The internal consistency on the activity items was calculated at .78; on the occupational stereotype items, .80.

In order to reduce the occupational ratings to single variables for a multiple correlation analysis, a factor analysis was undertaken (principal components, varimax rotation) of the occupations originally selected. Results indicated clusterings of these occupations into one female (female = secretary, nurse, housekeeper, elementary school teacher) and two male groups (male-1 = automobile mechanic, taxi driver, plumber; male-2 = police officer, business executive, doctor).

RESULTS

Prior to assessing the relations of the personality and activity ratings with occupational ratings, it was useful to examine the mean scores on the latter variable (Table 7.1). As would be expected from their clusterings found in the factor analyses, stereotype ratings by both boys and girls across the three occupational categories differed from each other. Although within occupational categories boys and girls did not differ significantly on ratings of female and male-2 occupations, the means did reveal a substantial difference on the male-1 category. Here it appeared that while boys see the jobs of mechanic, taxi driver, and plumber as mainly held by males, girls see them as held by both sexes.

TABLE 7.1

Means of Stereotype Ratings for Occupations

| Rater Sex | Female | Male-1 | Male-2 |
|-----------|--------|--------|--------|
| Boy | $2.19_a$ * | $4.13_d$ | $3.50_c$ |
| Girl | $2.24_a$ | $2.91_b$ | $3.26_c$ |

1 = females only.
5 = males only.

*Means with common alphabetical subscripts are not significantly ($p < .05$ by $F$ test) different from each other.

The main analyses involved calculating the multiple correlation of scales in each of the personality and activity categories of ratings with the above occupational ratings. The overall $R$'s, summarized in Table 7.2, were the basis for several generalizations. First, the tendency to see mainly females in "Female" occupations, the most stereotyped of the occupational categories, was significantly related to girls' stereotypes of their own personalities and of other boys' and girls' as well as their activity interests. By contrast, only boys' stereotyping of themselves with "male" activity interests was related to seeing females in "female" occupations. This was part of a major generalization that these activity interests were the only ratings from boys to be related to the stereotyping of adult occupations, and this obtained across the three occupational categories. The only exception to the above patterns was that girls with female-stereotyped activity interests saw mainly males in the male-2 category. Also of importance was that the magnitudes of these statistically significant relations between the sex-role stereotyping of immediate concepts and adult occupations were small to modest in range.

TABLE 7.2

Multiple Correlations (R) of Sex-Role Personality
and Activity Ratings with Sex Appropriate
for Occupations

| Occupation | Stereotype Rating | | | | | |
| | Of Self | | Of Others | | Of Activity Interests | |
| | Boys | Girls | Boys | Girls | Boys | Girls |
|---|---|---|---|---|---|---|
| Female: secretary, nurse, housekeeper, schoolteacher | .40 | .44* | .30 | .54* | .43* | .43* |
| Male-1: mechanic, taxi driver, plumber | .24 | .24 | .33 | .36 | .41* | .35 |
| Male-2: police officer, executive, doctor | .16 | .25 | .26 | .39 | .43* | .39* |

*$p < .05$

DISCUSSION

One key pattern of the results is that even when relations can
be found between children's sex-role stereotyping of personalities
and activities with occupations, there are differences according to
the sex of child as well as the occupational stereotype. As seen in
Table 7.1, girls were more inclined to mix males and females in
the male-1 occupations than were boys, but both saw mainly women
in the female ones. The latter sex-role bias was also the one most
related to girls' sex-role stereotyping of themselves on the other
concepts. It could be implied that if the girls were now making a
"breakthrough" in occupational sex-role attitudes, it is in seeing
females in traditionally male occupations but not males in female
ones. Boys, by contrast, seemed to harbor sex-role biases for
both male and female occupations, but such bias could only be related to their activity interests. Finally, across boys and girls,
activity interests were more related to occupational sex-role stereotyping than were personality characterizations. Perhaps this is because activities are a much less abstract manifestation of immediate
experience than are personality characteristics. Results could also

have reflected the problems with the personality scales as discussed in Chapter 5 (low reliability, questionable validity).

In the broadest respect, we again found only a modest relation among different domains of children's stereotyped judgments, and these varied with the sex of the children as well as the concepts. The problem of the scale reliability of the personality ratings of "self" and the abstract nature of the personality ratings have previously been mentioned as reasons for the low-to-modest correlations. On the other hand, the reliabilities of activity and occupational ratings were relatively high, yet the relation between the two domains was only modest. This again added to our doubts that sex-role stereotyping was a fundamental mediator in the children's judgments. Instead, it appeared to be a more particularistic bias that revealed itself on certain scales for certain children. As Spence and Helmreich (1979a) have suggested, there may be many "androgyns," and our data suggest that this may be true of children as well as adults.

# 8

# CHILDREN'S REACTIONS TO
# COUNTERSTEREOTYPIC
# TELEVISION CHARACTERS

The present study represented an extension of the last several chapters in that it involved the investigation of the relations among sex-role attitudes in different concept domains. In this case, the new domain to be studied comprised television characters who had been specifically developed to portray in an attractive and persuasive manner certain nontraditional sex-typed behaviors. This included, for example, a man who was markedly nurturant and a young girl who took charge of events in a confrontation between a group of young boys and a group of girls.

On one level, this was a study to see how (or if) our general conceptualization of a psychological consistency model would be borne out in children's reactions to the pilot television materials. In this general thinking, the media strategy for combating sex-role stereotyping was to present children with persuasive evidence that males and females could engage in counterstereotypical sex-role behavior. In fact, the plan for the first pilot of the "Freestyle" series (which was called "The Mike Farrell Show" and eventually distributed as a "special" with the final series) was to present a rapid-fire series of program segments, each of which portrayed nontraditional behaviors. This series included, for example, a song-and-dance sequence about fighting stereotyping, a put-down of a "macho" boy, and many examples of males and females in non-traditional roles (women executive, male nurse, and so on). The television production treatment was fast paced, light, humorous, and much more theatrical than documentary.

In terms of a consistency or balance theory approach, the television segments were meant to directly combat the children's biases about which sex populated certain occupations, the value of being "macho," the fact that girls usually let the boys take charge in situations, and so on. Given sufficient exposure to the counter-examples, the question was whether children's sex-role attitudes would then begin to reflect them. An even more immediate formative evaluation question was whether the children would initially comprehend the message in these materials. In view of the massive amounts of sex-role stereotyping found in typical television fare, would the children even be aware that the "Freestyle" characters were somehow different? This raised the further concern of whether we might encounter problems of selective perception. That is, would the children interpret these characters mainly in terms of their own sex-role biases? Would they fail to "see" that the male was nurturant? Would they reject outright a girl's taking charge of a basketball game? If selective perception were involved in children's responses to these materials, then we would expect that their biases in interpretation of the pilot segments would be predicted from sex-role biases expressed in perhaps one or more other domains (such as, activities, personality stereotypes).

Finally, we were specifically interested in how all of the above factors might come to bear upon the degree to which a child would wish to model his or her behavior after the television characters. To what degree would a child express a desire "to be like" the nurturing male or the girl leaders? Research into the model phenomenon eventually became even more important to us in later phases of the research project (see Chapters 12 and 13).

In overview, the study involved the presentation of certain "Freestyle" segments to children from whom we had already gathered extensive data on sex-role attitudes (Chapters 4 through 7). Response measures to these segments were then assessed relative to the demographic and attitudinal characteristics of the children.

## METHOD

### Subjects

The children ($n$ = 666) were described in Chapter 4. However, a socioeconomic index (1 = lower; 5 = higher) was subsequently constructed, based upon the neighborhood characteristics of the school.

### Materials and Measures

#### Television Segments

Early in the project, a series of audience objectives was formulated as a basis for designing the first television pilot. Guided by the objectives, television segments were intended to combat sex-role stereotypes through characters who incorporated selected counterstereotypical qualities. Segments in which these characters appeared included the objectives of children perceiving the limiting effects of sex-role stereotyping, females taking risks, female leaders, male nurturance. Main characters exhibiting these qualities were as follows:

Mike Farrell, a cast member of the M*A*S*H television series, appeared in a number of sequences as an adult male who could mix "gentleness" with "strength" and "leadership" with "nurturance."

Jeff, a teenage Anglo male, appeared in segments portraying counterstereotypical male behavior (for example, showing that it was okay for boys to hold dolls or spoofing the "macho" image).

Butterfly McMean was a young Black girl in an animated sequence who portrayed leadership and strength as well as a "feminine" interest in flowers and dolls.

The basketball girl was a young Black child intended to portray how a girl could take charge even when it meant taking risks. She was shown as a leader in a girl's basketball game that took on and beat a boy's group.

These characterizations were of particular interest to us as a basis for seeing if young viewers did indeed perceive the counterstereotypical qualities and, further, if children would express an interest in being like (that is, identifying with) the characters.

## Media Response Measures

Two types of comprehension measures, a "liking" scale, and four questions on how much a child desired to be like certain characters constituted the main measures used to evaluate children's responses to the television segments. Children were also asked to rate the aforementioned characters in terms of sex-stereotyped scales.

Comprehension questions were multiple choice (four alternatives) based either upon the children's interpretations of what the scene was trying to teach them (comprehension of objectives) or simply their recall of something observed or heard in the scene (factual recall). Liking of segments was obtained by using five-alternative ("I liked it very much" to "I disliked it very much") multiple choice questions on a Likert-type scale. Earlier, it was found that a Bugs Bunny cartoon would be rated between 1.0 and 2.0 on this scale as contrasted with a presumably boring segment from a soap opera that would be rated between 3.0 and 4.0.

Modeling intentions—that is, the desire "to be like"—were gauged in terms of a five-alternative scale. For example: "How much would you like to be like Mike Farrell?" Responses ranged from "like very much" to "dislike very much." Items were pretested for understandability; reliability estimates for combined measures were typically .60 or greater.

## Attitude Measures

The measures discussed in Chapters 4 through 7 were employed in the present analyses but in the reduced forms described as follows:

1. The Guttentag and Bray (1976) personality scales in the present analyses were those found most reliable (for example, internal consistency reliability of .60 or better) and that showed some preliminary evidence of correlation with the media response measures.

2. Activity interests were taken mostly from prior studies (Holland, 1974; Rosenberg & Sutton-Smith, 1959, 1960) where interests in various activities were used as a basis for differentiating boy and girl activity stereotypes. The same reduced set of scales was described in Chapter 6. The internal consistency reliability, represented by an alpha coefficient, was .78.

3. Children had also been asked the likelihood that they, "most boys," or "most girls" might engage in certain activities. These items were presented in multiple choice form where an activity (such as, "Most girls would babysit") was presented; then the child was asked to make a choice from five alternatives ranging from "agree very much" to "disagree very much." Reliability was similar to activity interests.

4. Job stereotypes were based upon prior approaches (Iglitzin, 1972; Schlossberg & Goodman, 1972) in which individuals were asked the degree to which men or women could perform specific jobs. These were the same as described in Chapter 7. Internal consistency was estimated at .80 with items rescored to a high score equal to a stereotyped response.

5. Of the personality stereotype scales discussed earlier, several were administered to gauge perception of characterizations in the media segments. Scale selection was based upon a trait that was to be presented in a counterstereotypical fashion. For example, the stereotyped adjective for girls would be "gentle." The intended portrayal was to run counter to this stereotype, but not so far as to be markedly "rough." Although these might properly be classed as media response variables, they were considered more as mediating variables than dependent variables for present purposes. Analysis

of these mediating variables indicated whether viewers actually perceived the "Freestyle" characters to be counterstereotypical; in this fashion, these variables served as predictors of reactions to the materials as well as of the utlimate effects of the television series.

## Procedure

Data gathering was undertaken in four waves. The first two were administered in the children's classrooms and required approximately 45 minutes each; the second two were undertaken in an audience-response facility and took about 90 minutes each. The test administrator read the material aloud, both to aid children with reading problems and to set the pace for completing the instruments. In classes with Spanish-speaking children, a bilingual aide assisted in explaining or translating items which might present difficulty. Video segments were shown on two 21-inch color television monitors, and responses obtained immediately after exposure.

## RESULTS

### Responses to the Media Segments

Scores on the media response variables were each subjected to analyses of variance of their overall means (To what degree did the children like, understand, or identify with the materials?) on variations by child sex, grade, and ethnicity. Means and mean comparisons from these analyses are summarized in Table 8.1.

### Liking

All subgroups of children rated the program material well in the "likable" range of the ratings. Females rated it more liked than males, Blacks and Hispanics more than Anglos, and fourth graders more than fifth or sixth graders.

### Comprehension

Success on questions directly tied to the objectives averaged 50.8 percent across all children. In the absence of significant interactions, main effect differences among the subgroups of children showed that girls did better than boys, Anglos better than Blacks and Hispanics, and compression did increase somewhat with grade level. By contrast, the children's average scores across

TABLE 8.1

Means of Media Response Measures

(in percent)

| Measure | Overall | Male | Female | Anglo | Black | Hispanic | Fourth | Fifth | Sixth |
|---|---|---|---|---|---|---|---|---|---|
| Liking of program (1 = high; 5 = low) | 1.95 | $2.09_b$ | $1.83_a$ | $2.35_b$ | $1.62_a$ | $1.89_a$ | $1.82_a$ | $2.03_b$ | $2.00_b$ |
| Objective comprehension | 50.80 | $48.20_a$ | $53.40_b$ | $57.80_b$ | $48.80_a$ | $45.80_a$ | $43.70_a$ | $52.70_b$ | $56.60_c$ |
| Factual comprehension | 88.10 | $87.00_a$ | $89.20_b$ | $90.20_b$ | $89.30_b$ | $84.80_a$ | $85.50_a$ | $88.50_b$ | $90.40_b$ |
| Be like Mike Farrell (1 = be like; 5 = not be like) | 2.97 | 2.91 | 3.03 | 3.05 | 3.08 | 2.78 | 2.85 | 3.18 | 2.88 |
| Be like Jeff | 3.38 | $3.16_a$ | $3.59_b$ | 3.37 | 3.42 | 3.34 | 3.37 | 3.40 | 3.35 |
| Be like Butterfly | 3.20 | $3.68_b$ | $2.71_a$ | 3.24 | 3.32 | 3.04 | 3.23 | 3.32 | 3.03 |
| Be like basketball girl | 3.78 | $3.93_b$ | $3.63_a$ | 3.30 | 3.15 | 3.08 | 3.32 | 2.97 | 3.25 |

Note: Within a main effects comparison (for example, within child sex), means with common subscripts are not significantly ($p < .05$) different by the Least Significance Difference Test (Nie, Hull, Jenkins, Steinbrenner, & Brent, 1975).

80

questions involving simple recall of segment facts were high (88 percent). Anglo and Black children scored higher than the Hispanic subgroups. A significant interaction between sex and grade was contributed mainly by averages from girls who did better according to grade.

## Modeling Intentions

The means of these measures were largely in the midrange of the 5-point scale, which would suggest that on the average children were neutral on their intentions to model the four key characters. However, the relatively large standard deviations (nearly half of the mean in all cases) indicated that individual children did vary substantially in how they responded. There was a slight (and expected) bias of boys wanting to imitate male characters more than females and girls modeling females. In two cases, there were significant interactions between children's sex and race. In modeling intentions for both Jeff and Butterfly, there were greater differences among girls in the three ethnic groups than among boys. For Jeff, Anglo and Hispanic girls indicated slightly greater identification (both 3.47) than did Black girls (3.83). There was a similar pattern in identification with Butterfly (Black girls = 3.03; Anglo = 2.80; Hispanic = 2.30).

## Correlates of Responses to the Materials

The second set of analyses was focused upon the examination of the attitudinal correlates of the responses. As mentioned earlier, a variety of attitudinal measures, mostly based upon prior studies of sex-role stereotyping, had been employed with the present children. In simplest form, the question was whether such attitudes were related to liking of the program, and objective and factual comprehension, as well as modeling intentions for four of the characters.

An earlier overall factor analysis was used as a basis for reducing the attitudinal instruments to a set of variables fewer than their individual scales (which had considerable multicollinearity). The polarity of the scales was also aligned so that a high score would indicate a high stereotype bias. Thus the Guttentag and Bray personality ratings were reduced to three variables, "male stereotype," "female stereotype," and "self-stereotype," the latter on scales corresponding to the sex of the respondent. A high male stereotype score would indicate ratings toward adjectives of a male bias (such as, "rough"); a high female score, toward such adjectives as "gentle." Similarly, high ratings of activity interest or intention scales would indicate a liking of activities often associated with male or female roles. Job stereotype indicated the degree to which children saw only males or females or both in a given occupation; again, a high score would be a stereotypic response. Finally, for the personality ratings of the males and females in the television segments, a high score meant that they were rated stereotypically relative to their sex (or a low score would indicate a counter-stereotypic rating). The character stereotype ratings were summed separately for the two male and the two female characters.

The attitudinal relations were assessed by developing a multiple regression equation of each response variable on the attitudinal variables (in the aforementioned reduced form) but first accounting for the variance related to demographic variables. Because personality and activity ratings were felt to be the sex-role attitudes most supported by prior research as well as fundamental to the child's perceptions, they were entered next into the equations. There was no particular reason for the order of the variables within this group, and it ultimately made little difference. Since personality ratings of characters in the materials were thought to be mediating variables and also the most speculative of these variables, they were entered last.

The correlational results calculated with the equations are summarized in Tables 8.2 (boys) and 8.3 (girls). The multiple R for each group in the final equation is given in parentheses; zero-order correlations for the constituent variables are included for further reference.

## Liking the Program

Beyond relations with demographic variables, ratings of liking the television materials were slightly related to activity interests and more so to character stereotypes for both groups. For both boys and girls, an interest in female-typed activities, a bias of the program materials, was linked with liking them. Although the girls' ratings of characters did contribute further to the regression equation, the zero-order correlations were quite small. As for boys' ratings of the characters, the more they saw the female character (Butterfly and the basketball girl) as counterstereotypical, the more they liked the program. However, their ratings of the male characters correlated in a stereotyped direction; that is, those who liked the program rated Mike Farrell and Jeff with a masculine bias.

TABLE 8.2

Boys' Data: Relations of Demographic and Sex-Role Attitude Variables to Media Responses

| Predictor | Liking of Program (1 = high) | Objective Comprehensive (100 percent = high) | Factual Comprehensive (100 percent = high) | Modeling Mike (1 = high) | Modeling Jeff | Modeling Butterfly | Modeling Basketball Girl |
|---|---|---|---|---|---|---|---|
| Demographics | (.54)* | (.28) | (.10) | (.13) | (.10) | (.14) | (.19) |
| Black (= 1; other = 0) | -.45 | -.03 | .03 | -.05 | -.09 | -.06 | -.05 |
| Hispanic | -.01 | -.20 | -.08 | -.03 | .05 | .02 | -.03 |
| Age | .03 | .12 | -.06 | -.05 | -.03 | .02 | .01 |
| Socioeconomic (1 = lower; 5 = hyphen) | .34 | -.03 | -.02 | .12 | .03 | .13 | .19 |
| Personality[a] | (.55) | (.35)* | (.11) | (.19) | (.16) | (.18) | (.22) |
| Male bias | .06 | .17 | .03 | .11 | -.03 | .10 | .07 |
| Female bias | .01 | .16 | .03 | .06 | .07 | .03 | -.04 |
| Self-bias (male) | .21 | .07 | .02 | .11 | -.11 | -.01 | .13 |
| Activity interests[a] | (.58)* | (.38) | (.12) | (.26)* | (.18) | (.20) | (.29)* |
| Female activities bias | -.28 | -.16 | -.04 | -.21 | -.01 | -.09 | -.19 |
| Male activities bias | -.11 | -.09 | -.01 | .06 | -.09 | .03 | .13 |
| Activities intentions[a] | (.61) | (.41) | (.18) | (.29) | (.09) | (.20) | (.30) |
| Self-bias (male) | -.21 | -.02 | -.10 | -.07 | -.03 | .02 | -.03 |
| Male bias | -.17 | .01 | -.10 | .03 | -.06 | .02 | -.05 |
| Female bias | -.15 | .16 | .03 | -.09 | -.04 | -.01 | -.09 |
| Job stereotypes[a] | (.61) | (.44)* | (.21) | (.34) | (.23) | (.22) | (.33) |
| Female | .15 | .06 | .10 | .18 | .08 | .13 | .18 |
| Male | .16 | -.18 | -.10 | .13 | .10 | .07 | .07 |
| Character stereotypes[a] | (.67)* | (.54)* | (.43)* | (.41)* | (.25) | (.34)* | (.42)* |
| Male bias | -.22 | .28 | .32 | -.25 | .02 | -.02 | .00 |
| Female bias | .30 | -.23 | -.20 | .16 | .01 | .25 | .29 |

[a]High scores on attitude variables indicate high preference or bias on the variable.

[b]R (p < .05).

Note: Read down the column for the cumulative R in parentheses for the addition of each cluster of variables; zero-order r's are outside parentheses.

TABLE 8.3

Girls' Data: Relations of Demographic and Sex-Role Attitude Variables to Media Responses

| Predictor | Liking of Program (1 = high) | Objective Comprehension (100 percent = high) | Factual Comprehension (100 percent = high) | Modeling Mike (1 = high) | Modeling Jeff | Modeling Butterfly | Modeling Basketball Girl |
|---|---|---|---|---|---|---|---|
| Demographics | (.39)* | (.41)* | (.38)* | (.23) | (.16) | (.22)* | (.26)* |
| Black (= 1; other = 0) | -.28 | -.22 | -.02 | .13 | .15 | -.14 | .00 |
| Hispanic | -.08 | -.17 | -.28 | -.04 | -.10 | -.10 | -.02 |
| Age | .01 | .17 | .13 | -.09 | -.02 | .04 | -.02 |
| Socioeconomic | | | | | | | |
| (1 = lower; 5 = hyphen) | .28 | .19 | .20 | .13 | -.06 | -.02 | .24 |
| Personality[a] | (.41) | (.48)* | (.47)* | (.23) | (.18) | (.23) | (.30) |
| Male bias | .09 | .22 | .30 | -.01 | -.04 | .02 | -.07 |
| Female bias | .00 | .08 | .06 | .01 | .02 | .05 | .09 |
| Self-bias (female) | .00 | .23 | .19 | -.04 | -.09 | -.06 | -.06 |
| Activity interests[a] | (.46)* | (.48) | (.48) | (.27) | (.19) | (.27) | (.31) |
| Female activities bias | -.23 | -.17 | -.23 | .05 | .05 | -.12 | -.08 |
| Male activities bias | -.15 | -.07 | -.05 | -.12 | -.01 | .00 | .03 |
| Activities intentions[a] | (.48) | (.49) | (.52)* | (.31) | (.21) | (.30) | (.37)* |
| Self-bias (female) | .01 | -.05 | .06 | -.09 | -.02 | -.02 | .22 |
| Male bias | .06 | .00 | .17 | -.02 | .08 | .15 | -.02 |
| Female bias | -.06 | .00 | .18 | .05 | .05 | .04 | -.12 |
| Job stereotypes[a] | (.48) | (.51) | (.56)* | (.32) | (.21) | (.32) | (.42) |
| Female | .03 | .09 | .02 | .11 | .01 | -.01 | -.05 |
| Male | .01 | -.13 | -.19 | .06 | -.03 | -.07 | .11 |
| Character stereotypes[a] | (.52)* | (.59)* | (.59)* | (.37) | (.25) | (.35) | (.42) |
| Male bias | -.15 | .22 | .22 | -.11 | -.09 | -.11 | -.07 |
| Female bias | .04 | -.33 | -.19 | -.06 | -.03 | .03 | .14 |

[a]High scores on attitude variables indicate high preference or bias on the variable.

*R (p < .05).

Note: Read down the column for the cumulative R in parentheses for the addition of each cluster of variables; zero-order r's are outside parentheses.

## Objective Comprehension

Beyond correlations with demographic variables, objective comprehension did show a pattern of relations with character ratings. For both boys and girls, the more the female characters were rated counterstereotypically, the better the children scored in objective comprehension. (Note that the polarity of this dependent variable is the opposite of the former one.) However, seeing the male characters stereotypically was related to comprehension. Other minor contributors to the equations predicting objective comprehension were stereotype ratings on personality traits and boys' seeing more females than males in male jobs.

## Factual Comprehension

Factual comprehension was more related to attitude measures for girls than for boys. Again, the perception of the female characters as counterstereotypic and males as stereotypic was correlated with comprehension. Additional attitudinal correlates for girls included rating personalities of males as well as themselves stereotypically, less interest in female activities, and seeing more females than males in male-typed occupations (but mainly females in female ones).

## Modeling Intentions

On the whole, the modeling intention results were less than we had hoped for. Girls' modeling intentions were not predictable to any marked degree. The slight patterns did show some relationships: minority children tended to identify with Butterfly; lower socioeconomic children, with basketball girl; and girls who rated themselves less stereotypically female tended to indicate modeling of basketball girl.

Boys' ratings of modeling intentions were somewhat more interesting to us but still not of a marked pattern. Intentions to model Mike's or basketball girl's behavior were slightly associated with higher interest in stereotypical female activities, or else the opposite occurred—lack of interest in female activities correlated with lack of intention to be Mike. Modeling Mike was slightly correlated with perceiving the television characters as male, but modeling Butterfly and basketball girl were slightly correlated with perceiving the television female characters as less female (or vice versa). One interpretation here—and consistent with typical findings of boys' preferences—is that boys will tend to model malelike behaviors from either male or female models. However, results were too feeble to make more than passing mention of this point.

DISCUSSION

In all, the initial analyses did indicate that television segments specifically designed to communicate counterstereotypical
materials about sex roles can achieve some desired effects in children's immediate reactions. The materials did appeal to them,
and comprehension did increase somewhat with grade level. The
children's average scores across questions involving the simple
recall of segment facts were high. Anglo children scored lower
than minority children on liking, and Blacks and Anglos scored
higher than Hispanic children on factual comprehension. On the
other hand, the comprehension of questions specifically tied to sex-
role objectives was lower than we desired, and the desired modeling of counterstereotypic characterizations was mixed at best.

The relationship of responses to demographic variables did
show corroboration with the generalization (for example, Greenberg
& Dervin, 1970) that minority and lower socioeconomic status children frequently report a greater liking for television but tend to
get less information from it.

Additionally, girls seemed to be more receptive and to better
comprehend the counterstereotyped messages.

Of particular theoretical interest to us in the present analyses
was how children's sex-role attitudes might enter into their responses
to the counterstereotypic materials. The results did reveal several
interpretable patterns of attitudinal relations to the array of response measures. For example, if a child tended to rate the concepts of "most boys" and "most girls" in a stereotyped manner, he
or she also tended to do better in comprehending the sex-role
objectives of the segments. This is, of course, contrary to a
selective perception hypothesis. It suggests more that a child with
salient sex-role attitudes was more likely to get the nontraditional
sex-role "point" of the segments, even if his or her attitudes were
traditionally stereotyped.

However, upon further inspection we see that the boys who
rated the female characters as counterstereotypic liked the program
and that boys and girls tended to do better in both factual and objective comprehension when the female roles were perceived as
counterstereotypic. But when the male characters were rated as
stereotypic, the children also responded favorably on liking and
comprehension measures. These findings, by contrast, do reflect
a type of selective bias in perception of the materials, one centered
upon malelike behaviors. Stereotypic males and nonstereotypic females both shared a male bias in our attitude measures, and this
bias seemed linked with liking and learning from the program. We
do not know from our study whether this was a result of a bias in the

context of our television pilot materials or in the children's perceptual processes. If it is in the content, this tells us that the producer did a good job in presenting television characterizations of nontraditional females but a not-so-good job in presenting ones of nontraditional males. But if the bias is in how the children view sex-typed behaviors, this says that they may attend more to male behaviors and thus see them nontraditionally in a female's actions but that they may not see the opposite condition. Thus, getting the idea across that men do not have to act stereotypically aggressive (and the like) may be the hardest task of all.

Finally, the results of this study dealt a final blow to our early assumption that the key to changing sex-role stereotypes in children would be to attack their global notions of sex-role stereotyping with massive counterexamples. We did not find convincing evidence that such stereotyping is global at all; whatever existed seemed to interact with the sex of the child and the concepts being evaluated. Moreover, the present study alerted us to the probability that certain kinds of abstractions about sex roles (such as, that men can be gentle) might not be all that perceptible to children.

As developed in the next chapter, we turned to a conceptualization that would focus more on specific sex-typed behaviors rather than on personality abstractions.

# 9

## IF STEREOTYPING IS NOT
## A GLOBAL CONCEPT, WHAT THEN?

Even with the evidence in hand (Chapter 8) that children respond favorably to counterstereotypic sex-role characteristics in
television performances, we were nevertheless uneasy with a media
strategy that assumed that one could penetrate a child's sex-role
biases as a kind of central concept and thus affect a broad range of
attitudes and behaviors. As reported in earlier chapters (Chapters
5, 6, and 7), we had been unable to find evidence of strong relations
of stereotyping from one concept domain to another. Instead, it appeared as if sex-role stereotyping by the children in our research
groups were more particularistic than central and global. Moreover,
as one is often reminded in working with children, measures of abstractions (for example, personality characteristics) are not all that
valid and reliable. Our extensive interview work with the children
corroborated our feeling that expressions of stereotyping ("Women
don't make good truck drivers") were usually not evidence of deep-
seated biases ("Well, if they don't have to load the truck, it would
probably be OK"). Instead, children seemed to be evaluating individual examples of behaviors in and of themselves, not as a broad
concept class or basic sex-role bias.

The foregoing led us to search for a theoretical perspective
and hopefully a workable model that would place the focus upon specific behaviors and their determinants. If a male child said that he
would not babysit under any circumstances, what reasons might be
associated directly with his decisions? Moreover, we were seeking
an approach that would allow us to make specific predictions about
behavior change and to identify the influences that maintained sex-
typed behavior or that could be activated in the cause of change. We
needed to focus on specific behaviors, believing this to be consistent

with the particularistic Weltanschauung of our target audience and faithful to the more explicit aims of the "Freestyle" curriculum as well.


EXPECTANCY VALUE THEORY

Expectancy value theory (Fishbein & Ajzen, 1975) proved to be a heuristic paradigm for our purposes. Based on reinforcement theory notions, expectancy value theory posits two basic determinants of behavior: attitudes and perceived social norms. The theory is intended for use in the study of attitude change and makes specific predictions about likely changes, based on features of message content. The theory has proved successful in predicting variations in behavior and in generating suggestions for message content. Moreover, as we shall see, the paradigm offered the potential for studying the sources of social influence that constituted major project components, each of which could then be targeted by messages through the efforts of the various consortium elements—home guides directed at parents and school activities directed toward teachers and the peer group, as well as the television series itself.


FIGURE 9.1

Summary of Expectancy Value Theory


Attitudes—Personal evaluations
of the behavior

Behavioral intention—
probability of engaging
in the behavior

Perceived social norms—
what significant others
would feel about one's
engaging in the behavior,
weighted by motivation
to comply

As summarized in Figure 9.1, expectancy value theory assumes that behavior is determined by expectations of its likely personal and social consequences. The former, having to do with attitudes, consists of the individual's salient beliefs about the likely outcomes of a behavior, which are weighted by the evaluation of those consequences and summed over all of the salient beliefs about the behavior. Short of identifying all of the salient beliefs pertaining to a behavior, the individual's overall evaluation of its consequences may be substituted, an economy that was employed in the studies below. The influence of likely social consequences of behavior is found in perceived social norms. These consist of normative beliefs about whether important others want the individual to perform the behavior, weighted by the motivation to comply with important referents. These normative beliefs may also be summed over all referents or simply assessed generally for "all of those who are important to you."

Attitudes and perceived social norms can be combined to predict behavior or, more precisely, behavioral intentions. Behavioral intentions are, simply, the individual's belief or subjective probability that he or she will perform a behavior at some time in the future. Behavioral intentions, in fact, do predict behavior with some accuracy if the behavioral measures are taken a short time after the assessment of the intentions and if the behaviors measured are as specific as those in the intentional measure. Multiple regressions of behavioral intentions on attitudes and perceived social norms typically produce multiple $\underline{R}$'s on the order of .6 and higher, provided that the attitude and perceived social norms correspond exactly to the behavior designated in the behavioral intention measure. Some behaviors are predicted primarily from attitudes and are said to be under attitudinal control. Others are predictable from perceived social norms and are under normative control, while others may be under the control of both types of influence. Depending upon whether attitudes or perceived social norms are significant predictors, messages may then be targeted to the beliefs and affective relations (that is, evaluations or motivation to comply) that make up each and so induce behavior change.

Fishbein and Ajzen (1975) have argued that their approach resolves several conceptual and measurement problems that have long nagged attitude research, such as the failure to find high consistency between attitudes and behavior and the failure of attitude change to result in behavior change. The reader is referred to their work for a more complete discussion of these issues. At the same time, a major shortcoming is that expectancy value theory does not explicitly treat the influence of the mass media or of sex-role stereotypes, both central concerns of the present project. Therefore, it became necessary to conceptualize how these influences might enter the model. Following DeFleur (1972) and Gerbner and Gross (1976), the mass media may be regarded as definers (or cultivators) of social norms, portraying a version of reality that sets the expectation of viewers. Accordingly, we felt it appropriate to regard television as a kind of normative influence. We assessed normative beliefs about whether boys and girls on television would perform a particular behavior and gauged children's motivation to comply with (desire to do things like) behavioral standards set by male and female television actors.

We also found evidence that sex-role stereotypes might be properly regarded as normative beliefs, which, when combined with the motivation to comply with the standards for the behavior they imply, would predict behavior. We found that at least one group of researchers defined sex-role stereotypes as consensual norms about appropriate behavior for the sexes (Broverman, Broverman, Clarkson, Rosenkrantz, & Vogel, 1970). A series of relatively recent studies (Costrich, Feinstein, Kidder, Marcek, & Pascale, 1975; Snyder, Tanke, & Berscheid, 1977; Zanna & Pack, 1975) strongly suggested that sex-role stereotypes do set expectations for behavior in the course of human interaction. The invocation of a stereotype not only influenced the behavior of the perceiver of the stereotype but was found to have a reciprocal impact on the object of the stereotype in the direction of producing behavior consistent with it (cf., especially, Zanna & Pack, 1975). Thus, it appeared that sex-role stereotypes were indeed criteria for conduct that were standardized through interaction, which Sherif (1966, p. 3) identified as social norms.

In our subsequent research, sex-role stereotypes were treated as normative beliefs about specific behaviors referenced to standards for one sex or the other (for example, "most boys would [behavior]"). Together with the motivation to comply with the behavioral standard of the corresponding sex ("How much do you want to do what most boys do?"), we expected these beliefs to predict behavioral intentions, provided that sex-role stereotypes were in fact important to our target audience. With the elaboration of this conceptual approach, we were able to investigate patterns of influence on sex-typed behavior in our target audience. (This is the subject of the first study reported in Chapter 10.) We also wanted to know how these patterns varied among children with different sex-role orientations. We therefore conducted follow-up analyses (Chapter 11) aimed at distinguishing differing patterns of influence as a function of the traditionality of the sex-role behavior of the child.

IMPLICATIONS FOR MESSAGE DESIGN

Expectancy value theory also suggested several broad message strategies that could be used to change sex-typed behavior, depending upon which sources of influence proved to be the most important. For behaviors under attitudinal control, the strategy would be to change salient beliefs about the consequences of a behavior or the evaluations of those consequences. For example, if we wished to persuade girls to go out for football, we might find (and, in fact, did find) that an important—and negatively valued—belief about this behavior is that "girls get hurt when they play football." One message strategy that we followed in an episode was to change this belief by having the female lead character tell her parents that scientific studies showed that girls do not get hurt any more than boys do. Alternatively, we could show that getting hurt was really not so bad after all. In this respect, we showed our heroine "getting her lumps" but picking herself up and rejoining the fray. For behaviors under normative control, our intervention strategy was to show significant others who supported the target behaviors or to attempt to alter the motivation to comply with them or both. In one example, we had our female football star triumph over the backbiting town gossip with the full support of her parents. We also introduced a new significant other (role figure) for girls in this episode in the person of the football coach who ultimately backed up the heroine and gave her a chance to play. In terms of the expectancy value model, we offered a new referent and tried to make a case for the desirability of complying with his wishes regarding a behavior. In the special case of perceived social norms about sex-role stereotypes, our strategy was to portray a girl taking part in a "boyish" activity such as football. Alternatively, we could have tried to alter perceptions of the relative value (and hence motivation to comply with) of male and female sexroles.

EXTENSIONS OF EXPECTANCY VALUE THEORY

Even on a practical level of application, the expectancy value model offered advantages over the cognitive consistency approach by suggesting specific message strategies that could be readily realized by the television production staff. However, we felt it necessary to delve even deeper into the mechanisms by which program content might be transferred to the actions of our target audience. In particular, we were interested in television role characterization as a vehicle for carrying the "Freestyle" message. By contrast, most expectancy value research has focused on the effects of the verbal content of messages.

The work of Reeves and Greenberg (1977) helped to shape our initial thinking on this count. These investigators set out to chart the dimensionality of children's perceptions of television characters, further identifying attributes (for example, strength, beauty, activity, goodness, social support) that seemed to account for the majority of this perceptual structure. Although these researchers did not treat the problem of modeling explicitly, one of their so-called identification variables—"How much do you want to be like X?"—attracted our attention since it roughly corresponded to the operational definition of a behavioral intention to imitate the character. In the context of our problem, the character attributes that accounted for much of Reeves and Greenberg's identification dimension seemed promising predictors of the effectiveness of "Freestyle" characters as models for behavior.

This identification dimension was used as a basis for screen testing actors for roles in the final series, using the results to make recommendations about which actors would be the most effective models and what changes might be made that would make them more effective. At this point, we were also interested in the issue of how our characters might serve as models of others in addition to the self, since we were still mindful of modeling social influence relationships through our actors. Therefore, we also examined how some of the dimensions identified by Reeves and Greenberg might predict this sort of modeling—or social modeling as we term it— in the study reported in Chapter 13.

Reflecting on expectancy value theory, these efforts may be regarded as an attempt to manipulate a specific attitudinal influence. That is, we sought to create attractive and appealing characters. To the extent that our audience admired these actors, and also positively evaluated their actions, our subjects might be so influenced to imitate them. In terms of social learning theory (Bandura, 1969), these traits might be regarded as examples of model status cues, one of the proved determinants of modeling. Observers who perceive models with desirable status characteristics wish to imitate them because they believe that the model's behavior led to their enviable status, according to this line or reasoning.

It also followed that we should examine the modeling process with the purpose of better understanding how normative influence might be activated to increase effects. As described in the study on normative determinants of imitation (Chapter 13), the modeling literature suggested that the perceptions of vicarious reinforcement delivered to models by their symbolic significant others might foster imitation. This was all the more so when symbolic significant others were perceived to be similar to real ones with whom the observer was motivated to comply. Once again, there was a practical payoff in this research since we could now pinpoint flaws not only in the characterization of the leading roles but also in how those actors interacted with parent and other significant other figures that we had also taken some pains in designing.

# 10

## SOME SEX-ROLE CONTRASTS IN EXPECTATIONS OF BEHAVIOR

Initially, we sought to study how specific instances of sex-typed behavior were related to attitudes and normative influences and how such relations differed between girls and boys. The model for this study was Martin Fishbein's expectancy value theory, discussed in Chapter 9. Since to our knowledge the expectancy value model had not previously been used among upper-elementary children, we also wanted to see if the initial results made sense in terms of expected boy-girl differences and if children could satisfactorily use the scales. For example, we expected that boys would be more motivated to comply with what "most boys" do than with what "most girls" do, and the reverse for girls. We expected that boys would prefer traditionally male activities more than girls and would normatively attribute these activities to "most boys" rather than to "most girls." The converse should hold for traditional female activities.

Given limited resources, we could not sample the entire domain of childhood activities. Rather, we selected 10 activities suggested by the "Freestyle" curriculum planners as instances of sex-typed behavior. (The list appears in Table 10.1.)


METHOD

The 666 children who participated in this study are described in Chapter 4. These data were collected in the second of two sessions in the classroom, of which the study reported in Chapter 4 was the first.

Children rated 10 specific behaviors intended to reflect differences in a number of behavioral domains (for example, home, school, community, and play activities) in terms of their intentions to perform each. Responses were to the statement, "I will [behavior]," with each behavior substituted into the underscored blank in turn. Children were instructed to respond affirmatively (agree) if they now performed the behavior or intended to do it in the future. Responses were on a 5-point continuum of "agree very much/agree a little/I'm not sure/disagree a little/disagree very much." Additionally, a separate "I don't know" check box was provided. The attitudinal measures were responses to the statement, "What I think about [behavior]" (good-bad). Normative beliefs about specific referents (mother, father, best friend, teacher) were assessed with statements such as, "My mother thinks I should [behavior]," using the agree-disagree format. Children not living with their parents were instructed to answer relative to the man or woman who takes care of them. Normative sex-stereotyped beliefs were measured via agree-disagree responses to the statement, "Most boys/girls would [behavior]," as well as, "Most boys/girls on television would [behavior]." Finally, the motivation to comply with referents or normative sex-stereotyped beliefs was evaluated using a 5-point "want-don't want" scale on items like, "How much do you want to do what your [referent] wants?" or "How much do you want to be like most boys/girls?"

RESULTS

The first analysis was to compare boy and girl respondents in terms of ratings of the likelihood they thought that they might engage in the 10 activities (behavioral intentions) as well as their attitudes toward them. Table 10.1 summarizes the results, which indicated expected sex differences in behavioral intentions and attitudes as well as a close correspondence between the two measures. Being a baseball captain, playing basketball, mowing lawns, delivering newspapers, and building model cars were all evaluated more positively by boys than by girls with statistically significant ($t; p < .05$) mean differences. Working for an A in science, being a babysitter, doing gymnastics, and cooking dinner were likewise more positively evaluated by girls. Moreover, there were three boys' activities (mowing lawns, delivering newspapers, and building model cars) for which the girls' average rating was on the "bad" side of the 5-point attitude scale. "Being a babysitter" was rated on the "bad" side on the average by boys. "Working for an A in science" was more preferred by girls than by boys, suggesting that science may not become a male-dominated activity until later in school.

TABLE 10.1

Behavioral Intentions and Attitudes for 10 Activities by Sex

| Item | Bias | Behavioral Intentions | | Attitudes | |
|------|------|------|------|------|------|
| | | Boys | Girls | Boys | Girls |
| Be a baseball captain | (M) | 2.1 | 3.2* | 2.0 | 2.7* |
| Work for an A in science | (F) | 1.5* | 1.3 | 1.7* | 1.3 |
| Play basketball | (M) | 1.8 | 2.7* | 2.0 | 2.6* |
| Be a babysitter | (F) | 3.8* | 1.6 | 3.8* | 1.8 |
| Mow lawns | (M) | 2.0 | 3.4* | 2.2 | 3.4* |
| Do gymnastics | (F) | 2.8* | 2.0 | 2.8* | 1.8 |
| Deliver newspapers | (M) | 2.2 | 3.8* | 2.3 | 3.4* |
| Build model cars | (M) | 1.7 | 4.0* | 2.0 | 3.8* |
| Cook dinner | (F) | 2.9* | 1.2 | 2.9* | 1.4 |
| Be a club president | (M) | 2.3 | 2.7* | 2.3 | 2.4* |

(M) = male.
(F) = female.
1 = agree very much or very good.
5 = disagree very much or very bad.
*Denotes a significant difference between boys' and girls' ratings with higher mean asterisked ($p < .05$). Lower numbers indicate greater intention or a more positive attitude than higher numbers on a 5-point scale.


A further comparison of boy-girl rating differences involved analyses of normative beliefs concerning sex-role norms as held by "other children" versus "children on television."

Table 10.2 shows that children's beliefs about the sex-role norms of each of the 10 activities corresponded to many of the differences in male and female attitudes and behavioral intentions toward them. This held for norms applying to real-life girls and boys as well as to boys and girls on television. However, for "being a baseball captain," "working for an A in science," "playing basketball," and "being president of a club," girls perceived these male activities as being more typical of girls than did the boys. With the exception of "working for an A in science," there were no differences between boys and girls in their perceptions of the appropriateness of these activities as male behavior (that is, rating of "most boys").

TABLE 10.2

Normative Beliefs about Sex-Role Norms

| Item | Other Children | | | | Children on Television | | | |
| | Most Boys | | Most Girls | | Boys on Television | | Girls on Television | |
| | Boys | Girls | Boys | Girls | Boys | Girls | Boys | Girls |
| --- | --- | --- | --- | --- | --- | --- | --- | --- |
| Be a baseball captain | 1.4 | 1.4 | 3.6* | 2.9 | 1.4 | 1.7* | 3.4* | 3.1 |
| Work for an A in science | 1.9 | 2.6* | 1.5* | 1.3 | 1.7 | 2.2 | 1.6 | 1.4 |
| Play basketball | 1.4 | 1.4 | 3.2* | 2.6 | 1.3 | 1.4 | 3.2* | 2.8 |
| Be a babysitter | 4.2 | 4.2 | 1.2 | 1.4* | 4.0 | 4.0 | 1.6 | 1.7 |
| Mow lawns | 1.8 | 1.8 | 3.8 | 3.8 | 2.0 | 2.0 | 3.8 | 3.6 |
| Do gymnastics | 2.8 | 3.0 | 1.6* | 1.4 | 2.6 | 2.8 | 1.7 | 1.6 |
| Deliver newspapers | 1.7 | 1.6 | 3.6 | 3.6 | 1.8 | 1.8 | 3.6 | 3.6 |
| Build model cars | 1.4 | 1.4 | 3.8 | 3.9 | 1.6 | 1.6 | 4.0 | 4.0 |
| Cook dinner | 3.5 | 3.8 | 1.2 | 1.2 | 3.4 | 3.6 | 1.4* | 1.2 |
| Be a club president | 1.7 | 1.9 | 2.9* | 2.2 | 1.7 | 1.9* | 2.8* | 2.4 |

1 = agree very much.

5 = disagree very much.

*Sex difference significant ($t$ test; $p < .05$).

Eventually (Chapter 11), the real-life and television concepts of "most boys" and "most girls" were to be employed along with others as "significant others" in the prediction of behavioral intentions. The question was whether sex-role biases in normative beliefs would be significant predictors of biases in behavioral intentions. First, however, it was necessary to assess the degree to which children thought it important to comply with different significant others. It may be recalled that in the discussion of the expectancy value theory (Chapter 9), the potential contributions of beliefs about various significant others are weighted in the equation by separate measures of "motivation to comply." Our next analysis focused on these latter measures.

Table 10.3 shows that the motivation to comply with significant others differed between sexes primarily for sources of influence corresponding to the sex-role norms for that sex. That is, boys reported a higher motivation to comply with what most boys do, what boys on television do, and what men on television do, than girls did. Girls reported a higher motivation to comply with what most girls do, what girls on television do, and what women on television do than boys did. For teachers, best friends, and mothers, there was no significant difference in the motivation to comply between sexes. However, boys reported a greater motivation to comply with their fathers than girls did.

TABLE 10.3

Motivation to Comply with Significant Others

| Significant Other | Boys' Ratings | Girls' Ratings |
|---|---|---|
| Do what teacher wants | 2.0 | 1.9 |
| Do what best friend wants | 2.3 | 2.5 |
| Do what mother wants | 1.4 | 1.6 |
| Do what father wants | 1.4 | 1.8* |
| Do what most boys do | 2.1 | 3.4* |
| Do what most girls do | 4.0* | 1.8 |
| Do what boys on television do | 1.8 | 3.4* |
| Do what girls on television do | 4.0* | 1.8 |
| Do what men on television do | 2.0 | 3.4* |
| Do what women on television do | 3.7* | 1.9 |

1 = want very much.

5 = do not want very much

*Significant differences between boys' and girls' mean ratings (t test; $p < .05$).

As mentioned earlier, we did have response data from children where they had rated the degree to which significant others "thought they should" engage in each of the 10 behaviors. Because these results were the basis for a subsequent analysis (Chapter 11), because they were quite copious, and because there were no striking sex-role patterns over the prior analyses (especially Table 10.3), they are not presented here. However, there was a striking pattern of another type—namely, the uncertainty exhibited by the selection of the "I don't know" option on the scale. Presumably, the greater the uncertainty about the wishes of a significant other, the greater the potential to influence behavior through television content that portrays role models who support the behavior. Table 10.4 shows that the classroom teacher, followed by best friends, was the most uncertain source of influence. Up to 39 percent of the children said that they did not know the desires of their teachers relative to certain activities, with the expected exception of "working for an A in science."

Between 13 and 23 percent of all children did not hold a definite social normative belief relative to their best friends for these activities. Desires of parents were generally better known, although even here there was a sizable amount of ambiguity for activities outside of home or school. Best known of all were normative beliefs about what most boys and girls or boys and girls on television would do. Even here there were sizable amounts of ambiguity about whether counterstereotypical activities like babysitting and building model cars for boys and being a baseball captain, building model cars, and being a club president for girls are appropriate for those sexes. Of the activities surveyed, the greatest amount of ambiguity about normative beliefs existed for being a baseball captain, followed by playing basketball and delivering newspapers. Working for an A in science was the activity for which normative beliefs were best known, followed at some distance by gymnastics and cooking dinner.

There were also several sex differences with respect to the uncertainty over normative beliefs (results not shown). For best friends, fathers, and mothers (but not for teachers, most boys, or most girls), there was a significant difference in the number of "don't know" responses summed across all activities. Girls were more uncertain about normative beliefs than boys in each case. Although this could be a function of the predominance of male-oriented activities in the activities rated, it also indicates that there is a major opportunity to alter the normative beliefs of girls by providing them with new, counterstereotypical information about the sex appropriateness of childhood activities.

With these initial results in hand, we were relatively sure that we had a set of measures that were understandable to children

TABLE 10.4

Uncertainty Concerning Significant Others' Opinions
(percentage of "I don't know" out of total responses)

| Behavior | Teacher | Best Friend | Mother | Father | Most Boys | Most Girls | Boys on Television | Girls on Television |
|---|---|---|---|---|---|---|---|---|
| Be a baseball captain | 39 | 23 | 16 | 15 | 3 | 9 | 10 | 13 |
| Work for an A in science | 4 | 14 | 2 | 2 | 5 | 2 | 10 | 4 |
| Play basketball | 31 | 13 | 14 | 12 | 2 | 6 | 4 | 11 |
| Be a babysitter | 34 | 18 | 10 | 14 | 10 | 1 | 12 | 4 |
| Mow lawns | 32 | 20 | 10 | 7 | 4 | 8 | 8 | 10 |
| Do gymnastics | 23 | 14 | 12 | 12 | 6 | 3 | 10 | 5 |
| Deliver newspapers | 33 | 20 | 14 | 15 | 3 | 9 | 8 | 10 |
| Build model cars | 29 | 19 | 16 | 16 | 3 | 10 | 6 | 12 |
| Cook dinner | 22 | 16 | 6 | 8 | 11 | 1 | 13 | 2 |
| Be a club president | 29 | 18 | 20 | 21 | 10 | 13 | 12 | 16 |

and that sampled the domain of sex-typed behaviors to some degree. We next attempted to assess in more detail the patterns of influence on sex-typed behavior and how these patterns might vary according to the sex-role orientation of our subjects.

# *11*

# PREDICTABILITY OF SEX-TYPED BEHAVIORAL INTENTIONS

The purpose of the present study was to investigate how certain predictors of sex-typed behaviors might differentiate children in terms of their expectations to engage in those behaviors. Such an inquiry was thought useful relative to several of the long-standing theoretical controversies regarding sex-role development. For example, what is the relative importance of personally experienced reinforcement (as in social learning theory) as compared to relationships with parents (the central concern of identification theory; Kagan, 1964) or global sex-stereotyped cognitive schemata (as in cognitive developmental theory; Kohlberg, 1966)?

Several potential determinants of children's sex-typed behavior can be reasoned from social learning theory (cf. Mischel, 1970). Given consistency in reinforcement for sex-typed behavior, such behavior may become more and more regulated by self-reactions or personal evaluations. Another explanation for sex-typed behavior is that it may be influenced by social comparisons with specific others. Parents, particularly those of the same sex, are often studied in this regard (for example, Heatherington, 1965). Sex-role learning may also be heavily influenced by the peer group (for example, Brim, 1958; Rosenberg & Sutton-Smith, 1968) and by teachers (Fagot & Patterson, 1969).

Sex-typed behavior may also be determined by reference to normative beliefs about expected behavior of the sexes or about sex-role stereotypes (Broverman, Vogel, Broverman, Clarkson, & Rosencrantz, 1972). Studies with college-age subjects (cf. Snyder

---

John Ruchinskas is coauthor of this chapter.

et al., 1977; Zanna & Pack, 1975) suggest that the significance of stereotypes is to provide consensually acknowledged norms for behavior that are maintained through reinforcement given to members of the group to which the stereotype applies. Stereotypes, then, affect behavior to the extent that individuals are motivated to comply with the patterns of reinforcement implied in the stereotype (see especially Snyder et al., 1977).

The present analyses again utilized the framework of expectancy value theory (Fishbein & Ajzen, 1975), which is akin to social learning theory. It assumes that the intention to perform a behavior is determined by the anticipation of personal and social outcomes of behavior, corresponding to attitudes and perceived social norms, respectively. The relative contributions of these determinants of behavioral intentions can be assessed by entering them into multiple regression equations in which sex-typed behavioral intentions (BI) are the dependent variables and attitudes toward the behavior ($A_b$) and perceived social norms (PSN) are the predictor variables, so that $BI = w_0 A_b + w_1 PSN$, where $w_0$ and $w_1$ are regression weights.

On a practical level, this would tell us what kinds of influence (attitudinal or normative) might be most important in general and for the specific sex-typed behaviors studied. A further goal was to examine how those children who expressed traditional sex-typed behavioral intentions (boys mowing lawns; girls cooking) differed from those less traditional in their behavioral intentions (girls considering mowing lawns; boys who wanted to cook).

The foregoing questions were answered in terms of the two analyses next reported.


## PREDICTION OF SEX-TYPED INTENTIONS

The first analyses were conducted to determine the degree to which behavioral intentions of each of the ten specific sex-typed behaviors (Chapter 10) could be predicted from personal attitude and social norm ratings. Supplementary analyses were also conducted to assess which components of the social norm ratings ("mother," "friend," and so on) contributed most to the predictions.

Two sets of multiple regression analyses were conducted using the ten behavioral intentions (BI) as the dependent variables. Separate runs were performed for each sex since different predictions of behavioral intentions were expected as a function of the sex of the respondent. The child's attitude toward the behavior ($A_b$) and summed perceived social norm (PSN) terms were entered into the first stepwise multiple regression equations. The summed PSN included five significant others: "mother," "father," "best friend," "most boys," and "most girls." Each of the component terms of the PSN index consisted of normative beliefs about the desires of a significant other regarding the behavior in question, multiplied by the subject's motivations to comply with the significant other. The teacher as a significant other was not included in the analyses because of the large number (as much as 39 percent) of "I don't know" responses given by subjects. For other significant others, "I don't knows" were treated as neutral responses. Responses to all items were coded from +2 to -2 so that the most affirmative response ("good," "agree," "want") was scored +2.

The results of these first analyses are summarized in Tables 11.1 and 11.2. On the left sides of the tables are results of the reduced forms of the equation where only personal attitude ($A_b$) and the summed social norm (PSN) were included as predictors. On the right sides of the tables are results of supplementary runs where the social norm was not summed, thus providing estimates of the relevance of individual significant others in the predictions. For all practical purposes, these unsummed entries did not change the overall equations substantially; thus, such changes are not reported here.

For both boys' (Table 11.1) and girls' (Table 11.2 ratings, the results indicated that behavioral intentions in all ten activities could be predicted beyond a chance level on the basis of ratings of personal attitudes ($A_b$) and social norms (PSN). Also, in all cases, both personal attitudes and social norms contributed to the predictions, but not especially equally. For the most part (seven of ten activities for both boys and girls), ratings of personal attitudes contributed slightly more to the equations than did the social norm ratings. For purposes of description, we have included the zero-order (simple) $\underline{r}$ correlation coefficients in the tables. Since these are typically less than the multiple correlation ($\underline{R}$) in each case, it is clear that both attitudes and norms had unique contributions to the predictions.

To distinguish the social norm sources of influence for sex-typed behavioral intentions, the components of the PSN (for example, "mother," "father," "best friend," "most girls," "most boys") were entered as individual predictors of sex-typed behavioral intentions in a supplementary set of regression analyses. Again, for simplicity and because the overall equations changed very little, we have reported in Tables 11.1 and 11.2 only the simple correlations of the individual significant others with the dependent variable (BI) and have asterisked the values where contributions ($R^2$ change) to the prediction equation were statistically significant ($p < .05$). Here we found several contrasts between boys' and girls' results. For all predictions except "work for an A in science," the significant others of "father" and "mother" entered significantly into the equations. For girls, "father" as a significant other was more often relevant than

## TABLE 11.1

### Boys: Prediction of Sex-Typed Behaviors
### (values of R and r)

| Behavioral Intention | Mean (+ 2 = agree; -2 = disagree) | Overall R** | Predictor (r value) Personal (A_b) | Predictor (r value) Social (PSN) | Social Norm Component (r value) Mother | Father | Friend | Boys | Girls |
|---|---|---|---|---|---|---|---|---|---|
| Mow lawn | 0.89 | .48 | .43* | .32* | .26 | .33* | .14 | .15* | .12* |
| Build model cars | 1.22 | .57 | .46* | .44* | .42* | .45* | .12 | .13 | .06 |
| Deliver newspapers | 0.66 | .56 | .43* | .37* | .34 | .52* | .16 | .18 | .04 |
| Be a baseball captain | 0.78 | .49 | .40* | .36* | .36* | .33* | .18 | .26* | -.09* |
| Play basketball | 1.19 | .50 | .33* | .44* | .45* | .43* | .16 | .15 | -.06 |
| Be a babysitter | -0.72 | .59 | .51* | .46* | .43* | .40* | .14 | .18* | .20 |
| Cook dinner | 0.11 | .62 | .51* | .51* | .47* | .47* | .18 | .21 | .26 |
| Do gymnastics | 0.12 | .81 | .71* | .71* | .54* | .65* | .30 | .46* | .24 |
| Be a club president | 0.61 | .60 | .50* | .47* | .40* | .43* | .23 | .25* | .00 |
| Work for an A in science | 1.49 | .27 | .23* | .16* | .09 | .04 | .16* | .17* | -.04 |

*Denotes significant contribution to prediction equation ($\underline{p} < .05$).

**All $\underline{R}$'s are significant ($\underline{F}$ test; $\underline{p} < .05$).

## TABLE 11.2

### Girls: Prediction of Sex-Typed Behaviors
(values of $\underline{R}$ and $\underline{r}$)

| Behavioral Intention | Mean (+2 = agree; -2 = disagree) | Overall $\underline{R}$** | Predictor ($\underline{r}$ value) | | Social Norm Component ($\underline{r}$ value) | | | | |
|---|---|---|---|---|---|---|---|---|---|
| | | | Personal (Ab) | Social (PSN) | Mother | Father | Friend | Boys | Girls |
| Mow lawns | -0.35 | .55 | .49* | .52* | .23 | .28* | .09 | .15* | .07 |
| Build model cars | -0.93 | .53 | .37* | .40* | .37* | .35* | .04 | .28* | .26 |
| Deliver news-papers | -0.68 | .55 | .50* | .39* | .23 | .37* | .08 | .12 | .35* |
| Be a baseball captain | -0.25 | .63 | .53* | .52* | .34* | .39* | .06 | .19* | .33* |
| Play basketball | 0.28 | .56 | .48* | .39* | .38* | .34* | .00 | .18 | .20 |
| Be a babysitter | 1.23 | .55 | .49* | .36* | .27 | .29* | .14 | -.01 | .27* |
| Cook dinner | 1.78 | .36 | .29* | .25* | .18 | .21 | .12 | .00 | .17* |
| Do gymnastics | 0.99 | .60 | .52* | .43* | .43* | .40* | .11 | -.03 | .36* |
| Be a club president | 0.23 | .68 | .60* | .51* | .41* | .43* | .03 | .08 | .40* |
| Work for an A in science | 1.67 | .35 | .18* | .31* | .21 | .17 | .19 | -.12 | .16 |

*Denotes significant contribution to prediction equation ($\underline{p} < .05$).

**All $\underline{R}$'s are significant ($\underline{F}$ test; $\underline{p} < .05$).

"mother" in the equations. As might be expected for preadolescent boys' intentions, the significant other of "most boys" was more relevant than "most girls," and vice versa for girls' intentions. Likewise for girls' ratings, "most girls" as significant others appeared more relevant than did "most boys" for boys. Also it seemed evident that "best friend" is a negligible predictor as a social norm influencing behavioral intentions.

In summary, our preliminary interpretations were:

1. The behavioral intentions of boys and girls were readily predictable from ratings of personal attitudes and social norms relative to those intentions.

2. Although both personal attitudes and social norms enter into most predictions, personal attitudes seemed slightly more relevant to the predictions.

3. Influential significant others for boys tend to be both parents and sometimes other boys but not best friends.

4. Influential significant others for girls tend to be fathers more so than mothers and also other girls but not best friends.

## DIFFERENTIATION OF CHILDREN WITH TRADITIONAL AND NONTRADITIONAL SEX-TYPED INTENTIONS

The foregoing analyses put the emphasis upon relations of personal attitudes and social norms to children's intentions to engage in a variety of sex-typed behaviors. Presumably, the relations that were found represented possible correlates of sex-typed behavior. Our next question was whether we could recast the analytic model so as to emphasize the contrast between children who indicated intentions to engage in traditional (as sex-typed) as opposed to nontraditional (counter to sex-typed) behavior. What personal and social correlates might best distinguish, for example, girls who indicated that they might mow lawns from those who thought that they probably would not? Our method was to differentiate groups of children in terms of the sex-role biases in their intentions; then to look for differences among the predictor variables of personal attitudes and significant others. Would differences in sex-role biases of behavioral intentions be predictable upon the basis of personal attitudes and thoughts about social norms associated with significant others?

The perceived stereotype of the sex-typed behavioral intentions had been gauged by asking respondents to evaluate whether "most boys" and "most girls" would engage in each of the 10 activities. The three behaviors of "being a babysitter," "doing gymnastics," and "cooking" were clearly expected of girls but not of boys. The three behaviors that were most clearly male sex typed were "mowing lawns," "building models," and "delivering newspapers." Subjects were divided into "high-traditional" and "low-traditional" categories by a median split on each of the six behaviors, using the intention to engage in the behavior as the criterion. Children in these categories were then used as the groups in a multiple discriminant analysis.

The discriminating variables, as in the earlier regression analyses, were the ratings of personal attitudes and the significant others, which were left as individual ratings. To these significant others were added ratings that the children had given of "most boys on television" and "most girls on television." Here we were interested in seeing if the social norms could extend to media experiences with sex roles. Separate discriminant analyses were conducted for male and female subjects.

The results of these analyses are shown in Tables 11.3 and 11.4. It is clear that there is an overall predictability of high-traditional versus low-traditional behavioral intentions, given information on the subjects' personal attitudes and expectations of significant others' attitudes toward the behaviors. Using the function derived from the discriminant analysis, which forms a linear combination of independent variables that best differentiates one group from the other, we were able to predict actual group membership at a significantly greater than chance ($p < .05$) level. The prediction of a subject's actual location in the distribution ranged from 70 to 89 percent correct across all behaviors for boys and girls, with a mean of 75.7 percent correctly predicted (compiled from both tables).

Further evidence for the predictability of the model is shown by the canonical correlations. All correlations were significant ($p < .01$). and ranged from .37 to .84, with most ranging from .57 and .66. The one small canonical correlation, for girls cooking dinner, can be attributed to the lack of variance in the behavioral intention measure for this behavior. The median value for girls cooking was 1.90, leaving little to be explained even after the median split.

In examining the pattern of discriminators of high- and low-traditional behavior, it is clear that both attitude and significant others are influential in differentiating these two groups. If nontraditional behavior were solely the result of ignoring sex-role norms, then attitude alone would serve to discriminate the two groups. However, in all cases, the child's attitude is supplemented by perceived social support from significant others, which is represented by the multiple significant discriminators in each equation.

TABLE 11.3

Discriminant Analyses of Boys' Sex-Type Intentions

| | Behavioral Intention Mean[a] | | Discriminant Function Coefficient | | | | | | | | Canonical R | Percentage Correctly Predicted |
|---|---|---|---|---|---|---|---|---|---|---|---|---|
| | High-Traditional | Low-Traditional | Attitude[b] | Father | Mother | Most Boys | Most Girls | Boys on Television | Girls on Television | Best Friend | | |
| Male activity | | | | | | | | | | | | |
| Deliver newspapers | 2.00 | -0.01 | .43* | .62* | — | .20* | — | .18* | — | — | .61 | 79.9 |
| Build model cars | 2.00 | 0.38 | .45* | .56* | .23 | — | — | .32* | — | — | .57 | 73.5 |
| Mow lawns | 2.00 | 0.11 | .29* | .45* | .18 | .40* | — | — | — | .17* | .61 | 73.1 |
| Female activity | | | | | | | | | | | | |
| Perform gymnastics | -1.60 | 1.74 | .45* | .42* | .14* | — | — | .17* | .08* | — | .84 | 89.0 |
| Cook dinner | -1.54 | 1.46 | .63* | .25* | .18* | — | .16* | .16* | — | — | .65 | 76.7 |
| Be a babysitter | -2.00 | 0.51 | .65* | .27* | .30* | — | .14 | .13 | — | .13 | .60 | 75.0 |
| Average | | | | | | | | | | | | 77.9 |

*Significant change in Rao's V (p < .05); t test between group means significant (p < .05).

— = no contribution to function.

[a]Response to question, "I will . . . .": 2 = very much agree; 0 = neutral; -2 = very much disagree.

[b]Standardized discriminant coefficients.

TABLE 11.4

Discriminant Analyses of Girls' Sex-Type Intentions

| | Behavioral Intention Mean[a] | | Discriminant Function Coefficient | | | | | | | | Canonical $R$ | Percentage Correctly Predicted |
|---|---|---|---|---|---|---|---|---|---|---|---|---|
| | High-Traditional | Low-Traditional | Attitude[b] | Father | Mother | Most Boys | Most Girls | Boys on Television | Girls on Television | Best Friend | | |
| **Male activity** | | | | | | | | | | | | |
| Deliver newspapers | -2.00 | 0.35 | .69* | .27* | — | .16 | — | .24 | .26 | — | .52 | 72.9 |
| Build model cars | -2.00 | 0.07 | .33* | — | .21* | .39* | — | .14 | .46* | — | .69 | 73.3 |
| Mow lawns | -1.72 | 1.11 | .65* | .25* | .40* | — | — | — | — | .16 | .59 | 73.9 |
| **Female activity** | | | | | | | | | | | | |
| Perform gymnastics | 2.00 | -0.32 | .68* | .31* | — | -.16* | .39* | — | — | — | .59 | 69.6 |
| Cook dinner | 2.00 | 0.15 | .82* | — | — | — | .45* | — | — | — | .37 | 81.5 |
| Be a babysitter | 2.00 | -0.15 | .76* | — | .25* | -.17 | .13 | — | .19 | — | .64 | 70.0 |
| Average | | | | | | | | | | | | 73.5 |

*Significant change in Rao's V ($p < .05$); $t$ test between group means significant ($p < .05$).

— = no contribution to function.

[a]Response to question, "I will . . . .": 2 = very much agree; 0 = neutral; -2 = very much disagree.

[b]Standardized discriminant coefficients.

The exact pattern of significant discriminators can be observed in Tables 11.3 and 11.4. Attitude was a significant discriminator in all equations and served as the single greatest discriminating factor in this set of analyses. However, its relative influence varied, depending upon sex of respondent and sex typing of behavior. Few sources of social sanction were perceived by low-traditional girls for female-typed behaviors, leaving attitude as one of the few factors that separated those with high-traditional intentions from those less likely to engage in such activities.

Attitude was also the most important discriminator of boys' intentions toward female-typed behaviors. However, there was a greater range of discriminators for these behaviors than in the girls' equation, indicating that low-traditional boys perceived more social support for counterstereotypical female behavior than girls did.

The perceived social norm for fathers was a significant discriminator for all boys' equations and replaced attitude as the single greatest discriminator when considering male-typed behaviors. Within this domain of behaviors, the perceived attitude of the father was the single factor that best distinguished traditional from non-traditional children, with attitude a secondary factor.

The perceived social norm of mothers played a lesser role, though significant for female-typed behaviors by boys and three of six equations for girls. Overall, there was a pattern of interaction between the sex of the significant other and the sex typing of behavior, with father most influential for male-typed behaviors and mother discriminating most for female-typed behaviors.

This pattern also described the influence of generalized sex-role stereotypes, operationalized as "most boys" and "most girls." "Most boys" significantly discriminated the low- and high-traditional boys on all male-typed behaviors, while "most girls" discriminated girls on two of three female-typed behaviors. The media sex stereotype of "boys on television" was a significant discriminator for four boys' equations, though equally influential across male- and female-typed behaviors.

In all cases, the means of the discriminating variable in the two groups were significantly different from each other ($\underline{t}$ test; $\underline{p} < .05$). Thus, each group viewed significant others as supporting their behavioral intentions, with high-traditional children perceiving their important others as favoring traditional behavior, while less traditional children perceived significant others as endorsing counterstereotypic behavior.

However, this perceived support by important others was weakest for girls engaging in counterstereotypic female behavior. While the high-traditional group perceived support from significant others for engaging in behaviors such as cooking, low-traditional girls viewed their significant others as neutral toward the behavior. While the means for important others were significantly different for the two groups, this difference was relatively smaller than the differences among significant others in the boys' analysis.

## DISCUSSION

The most obvious generalization to be drawn from these analyses is that sex-typed behavior could not be ascribed to any single source of influence. Children's perceptions that behaviors are stereotypically appropriate for a sex were supplemented by expectations of external reinforcement from specific referents and by personal reactions to sex-typed behavior. There was no entirely consistent pattern of significant other influence across all behaviors or even within male- or female-typed behaviors. Personal attitude was consistently the most important predictor of sex-typed behavioral intentions.

The relative contributions of attitudinal and normative influences on behavioral intentions varied across activities, as did the influence of specific significant others. Thus, the pattern of significant other influence for any sex-typed behavior would seem to depend upon both the act in question and the unique reinforcement contingencies that apply to it, as social learning theory would predict. The prominence of attitudes toward a sex-typed behavior in predicting corresponding behavioral intentions also argues for the social learning view, since attitudes are the result of past reinforcement history in expectancy value theory. We conclude that among the determinants of sex-typed behavior derivable from social learning theory, personally held attitudes toward such behaviors are the most important.

These results address certain previous theory and research concerning influences on sex-role development. Conspicuously absent were consistent patterns of influence from same-sexed parents or from internalized sex-role representations (sex-role stereotypes), as identification theory or cognitive developmental theory might predict. Perceived social norms for mothers and fathers exhibited comparable patterns of prediction for both sexes. Stereotypes tended not to influence behavior much at all.

As might be expected, both boys and girls referred more to their own sex's stereotype in forming behavioral intentions than to that of the opposite sex. Cross-sex references, however, varied between boys and girls. Boys' perceptions of the social norm for the female sex role was negatively related to their intention to engage in two male-typed activities, while the girls' perceptions of sex-role social norms did not correlate with their intentions to perform any of the female-typed behavior. At the same time, the male sex-role norm predicted females' intentions to engage in three male-typed behaviors. This would suggest that boys refer to the female sex role as an indicator of what not to do, while the girls use the male sex role as an indicator of desirable behaviors. This may be a reflection of the greater liberty that girls have to deviate from traditional sex roles compared with boys or of the traditionally greater value placed on the male sex role. In any event, there is no evidence here that sex-role stereotypes exhibit a strong inhibitory effect on behavior. At least for girls, the action of stereotypes may actually encourage some to take part in counterstereotyped activities.

One of the more surprising results of this study was the lack of influence attributable to teachers. When questioned about behaviors outside the classroom, children were apparently unaware of what their teacher would want them to do, as indicated by the preponderance of "I don't know" responses. Also interesting was the apparent unimportance of "best friend" as a referent for sex-typed behavior. These findings go against the argument that socializing agents outside the home are playing an ever greater role in socialization (Bronfenbrenner, 1970), at least for sex-typed behaviors.

In utilizing these results, the limitations of this study must be noted. The behaviors examined here represent a restricted subsample of the experiences of 9- to 12-year-olds. Measures on other behaviors from other content domains, especially those under less personal control, could result in differing patterns of influence. The social referents used in these analyses are also a restricted set. Utilizing different social referents (for example, siblings) could show different patterns of influence. Finally, the subjects, while ethnically and socioeconomically diverse, do not represent the universe of preadolescents.

Several major patterns emerged from the discriminant analyses, indicating possible differences in traditional versus less traditional boys and girls. However, the most basic finding in these analyses is that both high-traditional and low-traditional behavioral intentions are a product of joint attitudinal and normative influences. These analyses do not suggest that nontraditional behavior is a function of a child's freedom from normative influence but, rather, show that both traditional and nontraditional behavior are supported by correspondingly traditional and nontraditional support from significant others. However, a relatively positive attitude toward a less traditional behavior was present for girls with counterstereotypic behavioral intentions, and this attitude was accompanied by rather neutral social support. This suggests that girls who engage in nontraditional sex-role behavior may do so in spite of, at best, lukewarm support from their significant others.

Among these significant others, the father was suggested as the single greatest social influence, followed by the generalized sex stereotypes represented by "most boys," "most girls," and "boys on television." With the exception of "boys on television," these significant others seemed most relevant when the sex of significant other matched the sex typing of the behavior. The support of an opposite-sex parent would seem to be a critical factor promoting counterstereotypical behavior.

These analyses still leave open the question of how these perceived patterns or anticipated behaviors correspond to daily life. The actual attitudes of significant others toward children engaging in traditional or nontraditional behavior were not measured in the current analysis. Rather, we are dealing with the child's impression of what these significant others think. However, while we cannot tell if these differences truly reflect parents' beliefs, it is these perceived beliefs that may form the basis for children's daily actions. Similarly, in the case of generalized sex stereotypes such as "most boys," there is no one "true" belief that the child should reflect, but personal interpretation of the norm may be a critical predictor of children's behavioral intentions.

# 12

## CAN CHILDREN'S INTENTIONS TO "BE LIKE" OR "BE WITH" TELEVISION CHARACTERS BE PREDICTED?

At this point in the series of studies described in the preceding chapters, we had gained a number of new assumptions about conditions surrounding children's sex-role stereotyping. First, it did not appear to be a global concept as suggested in many prior studies. Instead, the tendency to stereotype an individual, an activity, or an interest seemed mainly particularistic, without a strong relation of stereotype biases from one concept domain to another. Second, there was good evidence that intentions to stereotype could be associated with personal attitudes and expectations of what significant others would think about certain behaviors. However, even when sex-typed behavioral intentions could be predicted, there were no major consistent patterns of influence mainly by personal attitudes or social norms or even major patterns within the social norms. Finally, there was some evidence that norms learned from television (for example, "boys on television") might fit among the predictors of stereotyped intentions. This was the departure point for the next study.

As discussed at the outset of this volume, despite the abundance of studies of television and children, there have been few attempts to conceptualize the link between television-image characteristics and specific influences upon behavior. There are many correlational studies but few predictive ones. Although we did not achieve the power of a fully predictive study of the television effects process, the present study was an attempt to relate our earlier work with behavioral intentions to the qualities of television characters and a child's thoughts about social norms for behavior. Specifically, we were interested in studying the predictability of a child's wanting to be like a given character (personal modeling) or to associate closely with—that is, be with—a character (social association or interpersonal modeling).

One prior focus of theory and research on the effects of television on children's behavior has been character perceptions that determine young viewers' modeling of television characters. A variety of such factors have been discovered including models' perceived similarity (Rosecrans, 1967), sex (Perry & Perry, 1975), race (Greenberg, 1972), the sex appropriateness of their behavior (Barkley et al., 1977; Wolf, 1973), and the reinforcement they receive (Bandura et al., 1963; Walters & Parke, 1964). One series of studies (Greenberg, Heald, Wakshlag, & Reeves, 1976; Reeves & Greenberg, 1977; Reeves & Lometti, 1978; Reeves & Miller, 1976) has attempted to reveal the basic dimensions of character perception that predict children's identification with television characters, including their intentions to behave like or model actors they view. These studies were grounded on the assumption that the degree to which a character is perceived to possess attractive or desirable attributes can predict the degree to which children will attempt to model that character's behavior.

The possession of such attributes may be said to exert an attitudinal influence on the viewer. Attributes that lead to a positive evaluation of the model (for example, attractiveness) or that define its status (for example, age) may lead the viewer to positively evaluate the model's behavior as well. The logic behind this is that the model's behavior somehow led to its (desirable) status. By replicating the model's behavior, the same desirable consequences are expected. In expectancy value terms, this expectation of positively evaluated consequences defines an attitude toward the behavior.

Research on mass media effects on behavior suggests, however, that social as well as attitudinal influences are important. In particular, reference groups to which audience members belong hold norms that may modulate mass media effects on their own personal behavior (cf. Katz & Lazarsfeld, 1964; Lazarsfeld, Berelson, & Gaudet, 1948). The media also model interactions with other social roles that may alter our expectations of others' behavior and ultimately influence our own behavior toward them (cf. DeFleur, 1972; Gerbner & Gross, 1976). Accordingly, the present research examined how perceived support from significant others may determine modeling of personal behavior.

Perceived social support for modeling was touched upon by the "support" variable in the Reeves and Greenberg (1977) study—that is, how much other people in the program are perceived to like a character. Bandura et al. (1963) also demonstrated the importance of depicting social support or "vicarious reinforcement," as they put it. However, such perceptions would not necessarily have an impact on modeling intentions unless viewers expect that their own significant others will react to their own behavior in the same way. Thus, social referent support for modeling may be better conceptualized as perceived support for modeling coming from the viewers' own significant others. Such perceived social norms have generally been found to be potent determinants of behavioral intentions (cf. Fishbein & Ajzen, 1975). We expected that perceived social norms for modeling would likewise affect modeling intentions.

Modeling is not necessarily limited to "doing things like" a character. Characters may also be perceived as models for "doing things with." In other words, they may act as models of social roles other than our own with which we interact in a variety of contexts. We may distinguish these simply as personal modeling and interpersonal modeling intentions. Social distance (cf. Triandis, 1964), or the desire to associate with others in a variety of social contexts, is a suitable interpersonal modeling criterion. Of interest is whether the same attributes that predict doing things like a character, or personal modeling intentions, also predict social modeling intentions, or doing things with him or her. At the outset, we expected that the determinants of interpersonal modeling should vary from those of personal modeling, depending upon what makes someone a desirable associate in a particular social context.

In the present study, children rated the degrees to which they would like to be like and like to be with certain television characters and performers videotaped for the "Freestyle" project. They also provided ratings of selected qualities of these characters as well as of the degree to which they thought significant others would sanction their being like or with the characters. The analysis focused upon predicting the two types of modeling from the latter ratings.

METHOD

Subjects

The subjects were 161 children from fifth- and sixth-grade classes in two Los Angeles schools. The schools were in multiracial lower middle class neighborhoods. Subjects were split into two groups of approximately equal size, with each group rating half of a set of television characters so that all responses could be obtained within a single class period. The children were in the 9 to 12 age range.

Procedure

The data were collected as part of a talent test for "Freestyle."
Video tapes of two or three candidates for each of six major roles in
the series were made. Within each role, the candidate actors read
the same scene. Across all actors, the same foil was used as the
"other character" in each scene to hold constant the interaction effects between characters. Video tapes of the 14 actors were then divided into two sets of seven and shown in classrooms in the two Los
Angeles schools. After viewing each actor, the children filled out
a series of rating scales and made a forced choice among the actors
trying out for each role. All questions were administered orally
while children filled out questionnaires at their seats. Subjects
were told that their responses would be used to help choose actors
for a forthcoming television series. They were also instructed to
ignore the acting ability of the characters in providing their judgments, since the brief (one to two minute) sequences had not been
carefully rehearsed. Through these instructions we hoped to invoke the frame of reference usually used by children to judge television chacters and their behavior without resorting to well-known
characters with unknown and widely varying exposure histories.

Measures

Character perception dimensions were adapted from Reeves
and Greenberg (1977) and included:

Is this person good looking?
Is this person strong?
Is this person like most girls?
How much do you like this person?
Is this person like most boys?
How old is this person?

There were five possible choices for each of the first five attributes—for example, "very good-looking/good-looking/I'm not
sure/not very good-looking/not good-looking at all." For perceived
sex and liking items, the responses were: "yes, a lot/yes, a little/
I'm not sure/no, not much/no, not at all." Note that perceived sex
instead of actual sex was used since the roles were purposely designed to exemplify varying degrees of stereotypical sex-role traits.
Age was measured on a scale of "9" through "15 or older." "Liking"
was used as a general evaluative dimension. "Funniness" and "activity," used in other research, were not included since they were

not likely to be salient in the serious, static segments shown. Perceived reality, also used in earlier research, had proved not to be a major factor.

Consistent with the identification measure of the Reeves and Greenberg (1977) study, we operationalized modeling intentions such as, "How much do you want to do things like this character?" on the same 5-point scale ranging from "yes, a lot" to "no, not at all." Using the same side, the perceived social norm was defined as: "What about the people who matter most to you? How much do they want you to do things like this person does?"

A social distance measure for the interpersonal modeling intention was constructed using social contexts meaningful in the life of the child: "How much would you want this person in your family? As your friend? To play with you? In your class?" This measure was found to be a reliable (internally consistent) scale with alpha coefficients of .83 and above for both boys' and girls' ratings of both character sets.

## Analyses

Stepwise multiple regression was employed to assess the prediction of each of the two types of modeling intentions, personal and interpersonal. Separate analyses were performed for male and female characters and for male and female subjects, collapsing across characters. Separate analyses were also performed by sex. Thus, the "cases" were subjects by actors. For example, there were eight female actors, each rated by some 40 girls, yielding approximately 320 cases for these analyses, with the exact number depending on the number of missing cases.

## RESULTS

### Determinants of Personal Modeling

As can be seen in Table 12.1, personal modeling ("to be like" the television character) was predictable for all combinations of child and television character sex. In each sex-of-viewer-by-sex-of-character condition, the overall regression equation was statistically significant with multiple correlation coefficients ranging from .59 to .68. Next to the social norm ("what others would think"), the perception of "good looks" was the most consistent predictor of personal modeling intentions. As suggested by previous research, "strength" figured more prominently in the prediction of personal modeling intentions for boys than for girls. "Strength," however,

## TABLE 12.1

### Prediction of Personal Modeling ("to be like") Intentions from Television Character Characteristics and Social Norm Expectations

| | | | Predictors ($r$) | | | | | | | |
| | | | | | Character Qualities | | | | | |
| Sex of Children | Sex of Television Performer to Be Like | Overall Prediction ($R$) | Social Norm | Good Looks | Strength | Femaleness | Maleness | Age | Liking |
|---|---|---|---|---|---|---|---|---|---|
| Male | Male | .68** | .56* | .45 | .29* | .11 | .14 | .04 | .54* |
| Female | Female | .62** | .56* | .43* | .23 | .18 | .13 | -.04 | .42 |
| Male | Female | .59** | .53* | .37* | .27 | — | .31* | — | .39 |
| Female | Male | .67** | .60* | .40* | — | .33* | -.05 | .14 | .38 |

— = Variable failed to meet the minimum $F$ value needed for inclusion.

*Significant predictor (beta) ($p < .05$).

**Significant $R$ ($p < .05$).

was a significant predictor of modeling intentions only when boys rated male actors, and good looks was a significant predictor when boys rated female actors but not male ones. The perceived sex of the model was an important predictor of personal modeling intentions only when the actors were the opposite sex of the viewers. That is, the perceived maleness of the female actors contributed significantly to the personal modeling intentions for boys, and the perceived femaleness of the male actors was important for girls. The overall evaluation of the characters (liking) was significantly related to personal modeling intentions only for boys rating male characters. Character age was not a significant predictor in any equation.

Determinants of Social Modeling

As can be seen in Table 12.2, interpersonal modeling ("to be with") was predictable for all child sex and actor combinations. The multiple correlation coefficients were all statistically significant and were generally higher than those for personal modeling (.70 to .81). Social norms again entered significantly into all four equations, although their beta weights were uniformly lower than for predicting personal modeling intentions. Once again, "good looks" was a consistently significant predictor, but this time it predicted interpersonal modeling intentions in all four cases. "Strength" was not a significant predictor of interpersonal modeling in any case, not even for males rating male characters. The general evaluation ("liking") was the most important predictor overall, showing the highest beta weights in three of the four combinations of sex of character and sex of viewer. Once again, age failed to be a significant predictor. Perceived sex was more consistently related to interpersonal modeling intentions than to personal ones. Perceived femaleness had a significant beta weight when both boys and girls rated female actors as well as when girls rated male characters. Perceived maleness was a predictor of social modeling when boys rated male characters as well as when they rated female ones.

DISCUSSION

At the most general level, these results trace the consequences of considering modeling as an interpersonal as well as a perceptual process. Specifically, children's belief that their own significant others will support modeling was an important determinant of their intentions to imitate television characters with their personal behavior. Television performers may also be a basis for influencing

## TABLE 12.2

Prediction of Social Modeling ("to be with") Intentions from
Television Character Characteristics and
Social Norm Expectations

| Sex of Children | Sex of Television Performer to Be With | Overall Prediction (R) | Social Norm | Predictors (r) | | | | | |
|---|---|---|---|---|---|---|---|---|---|
| | | | | Character Qualities | | | | | |
| | | | | Good Looks | Strength | Femaleness | Maleness | Age | Liking |
| Male | Male | .71** | .50* | .53* | .30 | .06 | .32* | .06 | .59* |
| Female | Female | .76** | .45* | .63* | .40 | .31* | .06 | -.04 | .67* |
| Male | Female | .81** | .41* | .66* | .39 | .33* | .28* | -.18 | .73* |
| Female | Male | .70** | .46* | .60* | .32 | .33* | -.06 | .14 | .51* |

*Significant predictor (beta) ($\underline{p} < .05$).
**Significant $\underline{R}$ ($\underline{p} < .05$).

123

interpersonal modeling—that is, being with certain types of people. The present interpersonal modeling intentions were more determined by attraction to the actor and less by perceived social norms than were the personal modeling intentions. Modeling may obviously be determined, in part, by perceived social norms, but the process of learning about social relationships with role figures from television may differ from that by which we adopt models for our own behavior.

The present results also corroborate important aspects of previous research by Reeves and Greenberg (1977). Predictors of personal modeling of the previously unknown characters used here were similar to those found for the earlier sample of popular television characters. This implies the existence of a perceptual frame of reference that children bring to television content.

Similar to prior research, it was found that sex-typed biases in character perceptions may rely as much on the sex of the character as on the sex of the viewer. For example, "strength" figured more prominently in the prediction of personal modeling intentions for boys than for girls. However, it was a significant predictor only for male characters when rated by boys. Likewise, "good looks" was more important for girls than boys but did predict personal modeling for female characters when rated by boys. Interestingly, the perceived sex of the character was important only for opposite-sexed actors. This corresponds to the research of Barkley et al. (1977) who found that the sex appropriateness of a model's behavior, rather than the actual sex, was the crucial factor in facilitating modeling. In other words, boys imitate female characters most when the models are like boys. Girls tend to imitate boys when the actors are perceived to be like girls.

Some major limitations on these findings must also be noted. The sample size in the present study was small and restricted in its representativeness. The character set used here was limited to a narrow range of child actors. Different samples and character sets could well evoke quite different dimensions of character perception. For example, the lack of relationship between age and modeling intentions found here may be a function of the restricted range of age in the characters tested.

This research suggests that reference groups that may affect the modeling process should be studied in future research on the effects of television on children. For example, perceived norms about interpersonal modeling (for example, "The people who matter to me would like me to have this person as a playmate") might better predict social modeling than ones pertaining to personal modeling only. There would also be some advantage in resolving social support into component parts, that is, whether specific referent others would support social or personal modeling. These issues are approached in the next chapter.

# *13*

## VICARIOUS REINFORCEMENT BY "SIGNIFICANT OTHERS" ON TELEVISION

In Chapter 12 we saw how certain qualities of a television character were persuasive to child viewers in terms of their desires "to be with" or "to be like" that character. In theoretical terms, we considered such qualities to be one of the clusters of relevant variables in the modeling process. If a television portrayal is to motivate a child to act in a certain way, it should presumably symbolize: the behavior, the personal attitudes of the television character to be modeled, and the attitude of the "significant others" of that television character toward the model engaging in the behavior. The more that these symbolic characters are attractive (cf. Chapter 12) to child viewers, the more the children might then identify the characters' personal attitudes and significant others with facets of their own lives. To the degree that the behavior in question is explicit in the television presentation and that the linkages with the television character's personal attitudes and sanctions of significant others are explicit to the child viewers, then the probability should increase that the television presentation will motivate the child's behavior (or behavioral intentions). This goes beyond the more simple model discussed in Chapter 12 (for example, Reeves & Greenberg, 1977) where a child's identification with a television character was predicted upon the basis of certain qualities of that character. Our reasoning was that such qualities increase the probability of behavioral modeling from television. One major process by which this may take place is that identification with television characters affects personal attitudes and ideas about social norms relative to given behaviors.

In summary form, the probability of behavioral modeling increases as

The behavior (or intention) is explicitly perceived from the television presentation;

The television character is attractive to the child and personal attitudes toward the behavior are positive and explicitly perceived; and

The significant others are similar to those in the child's life, the motivation to comply with them is high, and their attitudes toward the behavior are supportive.

In the original study reported in the present chapter, several aspects of this modeling process were studied in children's responses to the motivational content of two pilot television programs from our early work with the "Freestyle" series. In both of these, a child was shown engaging in nontraditional, sex-typed behavior (a girl doing carpentry work; a girl joining a science contest).

There were also significant others portrayed in each drama, including mothers, peers, and, in one, a teacher. Given post-exposure measures of children's intentions to engage in these activities, what is the relation of such intentions to measures of (1) significant other similarity (for example, "My mother thinks I should do the same things her mother wants her to do"), (2) the perceived support of the significant other ("Did her mother want her to ____?"), and (3) motivation to comply with the significant others ("How much do you want to do what your mother wants ?").

PRIOR RESEARCH

Considerable literature already exists on the nature of vicarious reinforcement as an important determinant of imitative behavior (Bandura, 1969). When observers see models receiving reinforcement from symbolic significant others, this influences observers' performance of imitative behavior (Bandura, 1965; Bandura et al., 1963; Walters, Leat, & Mezei, 1963; Walters & Parke, 1964; Walters, Parke, & Cane, 1965).

However, the results are far from conclusive. Rosecrans (1967) found that vicarious reinforcement had no effect on modeling whatsoever. No single experiment has demonstrated the effectiveness of vicarious reinforcement over the entire range of this variable. Bandura et al. (1963) found more imitation when the model was rewarded than when it received no consequences and model-punished conditions. Others (Bandura, 1965; Walters et al., 1963;

Walters & Parke, 1964; Walters et al., 1965) found the latter difference but not the former. The inconsistent findings may be due
to the failure to examine the operation of normative influence in
studies of vicarious reinforcement.

In particular, prior experiments may not have altered perceptions of the permissibility of the modeled behavior, or normative
beliefs, as intended. Some may have employed symbolic significant
others so unlike real definers of behavioral norms—that is, having
such low referent similarity—that they had no impact. Also, subjects may not have been motivated to comply with the referents used.

Social norms or "criteria of conduct which are standardized as
a consequence of the contact of individuals" (Sherif, 1966, p. 3) have
long been recognized as important determinants of human behavior.
From a social learning perspective, vicarious reinforcement from
symbolic significant others should modify observers' perceptions of
the degree of support models receive from symbolic significant
others. The vicarious reinforcement contingencies may be said to
define the symbolic significant others' criteria for conduct (or social
norms) for the model in the eyes of the observer, forming a symbolic referent belief in the latter. This, in turn, may alter observers' expectations about the reinforcement criteria used by corresponding real significant others, or normative beliefs, and influence observers' own behavior. Indeed, the reason usually cited for
the potency of reinforcement administered by symbolic significant
others is that the consequences are cues indicating to the observer
the permissibility or nonpermissibility (for example, normative criteria) of reproducing the model's behavior (Bandura, 1965; Walters
& Parke, 1964; Walters et al., 1965).

The experimental procedures used previously may not have
altered beliefs about symbolic referent support. The disinhibition
argument offered by Bandura (1965) and Walters and Parke (1964)
refers to this notion. They attributed the lack of distinction between
the no-consequences and model-rewarded conditions to the possibility that observers perceived the absence of punishment for deviant
(aggressive) behavior to be as reinforcing as the presence of rewards. Similarly, Rosecrans (1967) attributed the lack of effect she
found to her subjects' misperception that reinforcements applied to
only part of the modeled sequence instead of its entirety. In a post
hoc study reported by Walters et al. (1965), the no-consequences
condition was altered to allow the adult reinforcing agent to stand by
impassively while the child model played—this in contrast to the
usual procedure in which no adult appeared. Subsequent interviews
revealed that the majority of the subjects thought that the adult dis-
approved of the behavior. Thus, the failure to successfully alter
symbolic referent beliefs as these experimenters intended may

explain some of the conflicting findings in vicarious reinforcement research. Mere exposure to vicarious reinforcement may not always alter such beliefs as desired.

A second explanation comes from contrasting the symbolic significant other used in the Rosecrans study, whose relationship to the model was unclear, with those used by Walters and his associates, where care was taken to make the adult appear to be the mother of the model. Vicarious reinforcement was effective in the former experiment but not the latter. Bandura (1965) used two adults, one acting as a model and the other as a reinforcing agent. Differences between vicarious reinforcement conditions were not significant for males as they had been for Walters's subjects, all of whom were male. Thus, a lack of similarity between symbolic significant others and real significant others (that is, referent similarity) for Bandura's male subjects may have led to the null finding. On the other hand, Bandura's female subjects may have been sensitized to punishment for aggression as a result of sex differences in child rearing. Perhaps the additional coercive power of real referents did not have to be invoked to affect girls' imitation of aggression.

Another explanation for Rosecrans's null finding is that her subjects may have been able to compare the symbolic significant other with a figure in their own lives, the experimenter herself in that case, but their motivation to comply with this referent may not have been great enough to induce imitation. In contrast, the motivation to comply with mother figures, as in the Walters studies, was undoubtedly high among most children. Even here the failure to distinguish reward and no-consequences conditions may have been due to combining children highly motivated to comply with their mothers with relatively "disobedient" ones. A variation of this argument is that the real significant others represented by symbolic figures may not have had the target behavior under means-ends control. It is noteworthy that Bandura et al. (1963) did induce the expected differences between reward and no-consequences conditions. Plausibly, the symbolic significant other used in that experiment—a peer reinforcing a peer model—had the requisite perceived control over the mutual play behavior modeled in that study. Perhaps adults have no control over play behavior when they offer positive incentives but do have when they administer negative incentives. In other words, children may not be motivated to comply with adults who reward them for play, which is not usually an adult prerogative, but may be so motivated when adults punish them. Thus, the motivation to comply with real referents should interact with symbolic referent beliefs and referent similarity such that the greater the motivation to comply, the greater the positive relationship of these variables to modeling.

In an attempt to resolve these problematic findings, Akamatsu and Thelen (1971) found that the reward and no-consequences conditions still yielded equivalent results when socially neutral (button-pushing) behavior was modeled, ruling out the disinhibition argument. However, Akamatsu and Thelen used two adults, one acting as a model and the other as symbolic significant other. Following the preceding argument, no difference between the two treatment conditions and the control groups might be expected.

In the present study of referent normative influence, it was anticipated that perceived symbolic support of significant others, or symbolic referent beliefs, would be positively related to modeling intentions over their entire range, not just at the low end of the range of referent support. The similarity of significant others to one's own should interact with referent beliefs such that the greater the similarity, the more positive the relationship between symbolic referent beliefs and modeling. The same should hold for the motivation to comply. Referent similarity should also be positively related to limitation. Adapting Bandura's disinhibition argument, the fact that a model performs a behavior implies the tacit support of his or her (symbolic) significant others.

## THE STUDY

Only certain highlights of the method and findings of the full study (LaRose, 1979) will be summarized here.

### Method

The research design, unlike most prior studies of vicarious reinforcement, was essentially post hoc and only quasi-experimental. After being exposed to one of the two television program pilots, children were divided statistically into subgroups on the basis of their responses to questions of referent similarity (Were the television significant others likely to react to the behavior the same as real significant others?), referent beliefs (Did the television significant others want the model to do behavior?), and motivation to comply with these significant others. Relations with measures of intentions to engage in the portrayed behaviors were then assessed.

The sample totaled 580 children drawn from 21 classrooms in six Los Angeles schools in predominantly middle-class neighborhoods. Table 13.1 summarizes their characteristics.

Each participating class was bused to a central auditorium where it viewed the stimulus materials. Subjects were randomly assigned to view one or the other of the two television programs. A posttest was administered immediately following viewing. Earlier (2 to 3 weeks before), respondents answered questionnaires in their classrooms concerning their media-use patterns and their perceptions of a variety of behaviors included in the modeling stimuli. Both male and female experimenters attended all data collection sessions.

TABLE 13.1

Respondent Characteristics

| Category | $n$[a] |
|---|---|
| Sex | |
| Boys | 315 |
| Girls | 295 |
| Grade | |
| Fourth | 221 |
| Fifth | 178 |
| Sixth | 209 |
| Ethnic group[b] | |
| Anglo | 257 |
| Black | 168 |
| Chicano | 154 |
| Asian | 33 |

[a]The totals do not add to 613 within each set of categories owing to missing data.

[b]Coded by observation.

Note: The figures are for those subjects present for pretest. Of the subjects, 89 were not present for the pretest but did attend viewing sessions.

One 30-minute television program called "Partners" was about a boy and a girl who started their own fix-it business and was intended to teach the merits of cooperation. Along the way, the girl modeled a variety of repair and construction skills, including a long opening sequence in which she showed her friend how to build some bookshelves and that served as the main focus of study. Her mother and her partner were the significant others studied for this activity.

The second program, also 30 minutes ("Cheers"), was about a boy and a girl who learned to be independent of the social demands of parents and peers and successfully competed in a science contest. Here the girl modeled an interest in science along with a (competing) interest in cheerleading. Her mother, girlfriends, and teachers were studied as symbolic significant others for the behavior of entering a science contest.

## Results

The distributions of children's responses to the referent belief and similarity measures were averaged across the respective significant others in the two programs. The shape of the combined distributions allowed a division of the children into three response groups for each of the two measures. These were then referred to as the "high," "medium," and "low" groups for ratings of either the degree to which a significant other wanted the character to do the behavior (belief) or the degree to which model's significant others were expected to react like the observer's own (similarity). In the first analyses, these served as independent variables, so to speak, while measures of the intention to engage in the two behaviors were the dependent variables. Separate analyses were conducted for responses to the two programs. Stepwise analysis of variance was used to correct for the effects of unequal cell sizes.

For present purposes, the results are best illustrated, first, in terms of differences in modeling intentions according to variations in the belief and similarity measures. Following this is an assessment of these differences in interaction with one another and with the motivation to comply measures that were also used to divide the children into three analysis groups.

Differences according to belief and similarity measures are summarized in Table 13.2. Here the pattern is quite clear. The higher the similarity ratings, the greater the intention to engage in the portrayed behavior, a result in accordance with our expectations. The main contrast, however, was statistically significant ($p < .05$) only between the high and the medium or low groups. A similar pattern prevailed for measures of belief, except that the differences in response to the "Cheers" program were not statistically significant. The pattern indicated that the higher the rated belief that a significant other was sanctioning a behavior, the greater the modeling intention.

Both sets of results were in line with our expectations, but perhaps with not as great a difference in modeling intentions as we had expected.

TABLE 13.2

Differences in Modeling Intentions According to Variations
in Perceived Beliefs of Television Significant Others
and Similarity to One's Own Significant Others

| Belief and Similarity Subgroup | Modeling Intention | |
|---|---|---|
| | "Partners": Build a Bookshelf | "Cheers": Join a Science Contest |
| Belief: Do the television significant others want her to _____ ? | | |
| High | $3.43_a$* | $4.03_a$ |
| Medium | $3.10_b$ | $3.49_a$ |
| Low | $2.80_b$ | $3.19_a$ |
| Similarity: Are the significant others like my own? | | |
| High | $3.80_a$ | $3.97_a$ |
| Medium | $2.94_b$ | $3.59_b$ |
| Low | $2.70_b$ | $3.28_b$ |

High value = high modeling intention.
*Means with common subscripts in the group of three are not
significantly different from each other ($p < .05$).

Do different conditions of belief and similarity combine in
ways associated with even greater differences in modeling intentions?
In other words, did the two variables significantly interact? The results of this analysis are summarized in Figure 13.1. The results
of the analysis of variance indicated a statistically significant
($p < .05$) interaction between belief and similarity measures only
for "Partners," not for "Cheers." With a minor exception, however, higher conditions of similarity or belief ratings combine for
the highest conditions of modeling intention ratings. Again, the results were in line with expectations, but differences in modeling
were not in great contrast with one another in the low and medium
conditions.

How does the motivation to comply with significant others enter
into this picture? What were the interactions relative to measures of
belief and similarity? The analysis of the variance indicated no
statistically significant interaction of motivation to comply with the

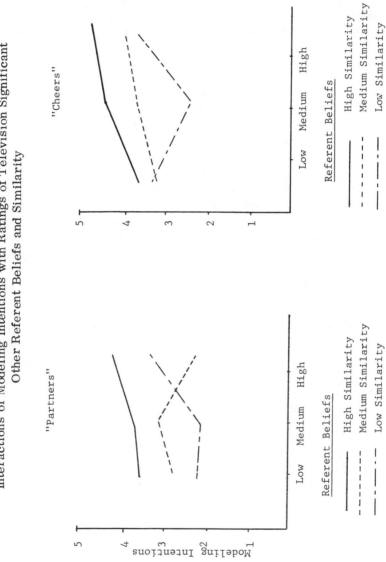

FIGURE 13.1

Interactions of Modeling Intentions with Ratings of Television Significant
Other Referent Beliefs and Similarity

133

belief measures. There was, however, a significant ($p < .05$) interaction between similarity measures and motivation to comply in the case of "Partners" but not for "Cheers." For purposes of comparison, the results for both programs are plotted in Figure 13.2. The pattern for "Partners" indicates a contrast between the low and high subgroups in terms of motivation to comply and higher modeling intentions, as referent similarity is rated high. But as the statistical analysis indicated, there is no such interaction in the case of "Cheers." The results are generally in line with expectations, but, again, differences in the low and medium groups were not marked.

Discussion

Variations in referent beliefs created by symbolic referent support, even those perceived by the observer instead of those intended by the experimenter, were not consistent determinants of modeling over their entire range. As in earlier investigations of the effects of vicarious reinforcement, negative reinforcement (low referent beliefs, in the current terminology) was differentially effective from positive reinforcement (high referent beliefs), but the contrast of these extremes with nonsupport (medium referent beliefs) was not as great as social learning theory might predict. The difference between high and medium support approached significance here, in contradistinction to many earlier investigations. However, the difference between medium and low support that was usually observed in the past was not in evidence. Both treatments may have had much weaker variations in vicarious reinforcement than the previous experiments so that the full range of expected effects was not found. Thus, symbolic referent beliefs may yet prove to be determinants of modeling.

The direct effect of referent similarity on modeling intentions was, if anything, stronger than expected. According to a straightforward social learning theory formulation, this factor should affect modeling only as it interacts with referent beliefs. A form of the disinhibition argument advanced by Bandura (1965) and Walters and Parke (1964) comes to mind to resolve this problem. Even when symbolic significant others do not offer overt positive reinforcement, observers may infer its presence from the fact that the model actually carries out the behavior in a way that would surely come to the attention of (symbolic) significant others. If the symbolic referent "really" does not want the behavior carried out, then it would not be. The permissibility of the behavior may be read into the situation by the observer and then the perception that "my referent

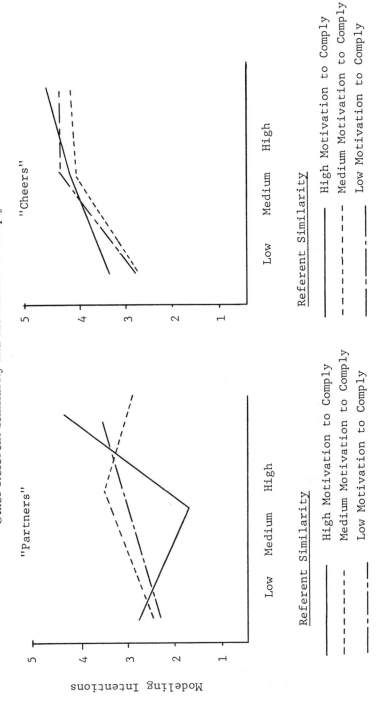

FIGURE 13.2

Interactions of Modeling Intentions with Ratings of Television Significant
Other Referent Similarity and Motivation to Comply

wants me to do the same things as her referent wants her to do" becomes tantamount to "my referent permits the behavior."

Symbolic referent beliefs did combine with referent similarity such that the greater the referent similarity, the greater the differences in modeling between lower and higher degree of symbolic referent beliefs. However, this was only true when comparing high and medium referent similarity. This implies that when a symbolic significant other is irrelevant—when it does not help to define what real referents do want or what they do not want—vicarious reinforcement is ineffective.

The fact that referent beliefs had differential effects on modeling within the low-similarity condition as well as the high-similarity condition was an unexpected result but one that may be interpreted readily within a social learning framework. Observers who believe that symbolic referents support a behavior and that their own referents do not, find the portrayal of the behavior to be especially disinhibiting. For them the portrayal of the activity may create an impression of its permissibility that they never before received from their own referents. The new knowledge that it is rewarded instead of punished may release them from the normative prohibitions that previously applied.

The motivation to comply with real referents appeared to act on modeling intentions only through referent similarity, and even then only at the extremes of the latter. When the motivation to comply was low or intermediate, referent similarity had relatively little effect on modeling intentions.

Thus, the motivation to comply with real referents enhances the effect of their similarity to symbolic referents. Perhaps low or intermediate motivation to comply indicates referents who have no means-ends control over the subject so that even if the symbolic referents are like real ones, they have no impact on modeling. A strong desire to please important real referents (high motivation to comply) may foster modeling only when it is relatively certain that the same rewards will apply to behavior—that is, when referent similarity is high. Perhaps such children are so "eager to please" that they will adopt a behavior only when they are sure it will garner the social rewards they crave.

The failure to find an interaction between referent beliefs and the motivation to comply has several possible explanations. For one thing, a general motivation to comply may not be an adequate predictor of a specific behavior. Likewise, the interaction might have been found if the actions of individual symbolic referents had been isolated and studied in combination with the motivation to comply with each, instead of averaging across referents. Finally, it is possible that children's motivation to comply may change considerably over even short periods of time, perhaps even during the two-to-three-week period between the pretest in which the motivation to comply was measured and the subjects were exposed to the modeling stimulus.

# *14*

# ON USING TELEVISION TO REDUCE
# SEX-ROLE STEREOTYPING IN CHILDREN

In Chapter 1, we noted that the TV CAP was launched when conceptualizations of sex-role stereotyping were undergoing a revolutionary change and when the use of television to promote prosocial behaviors was more a radical concept than it seems now. These points offer a useful organizing scheme for our concluding chapter since, obviously, if we were to be successful with "Freestyle," it would have to involve valid assumptions about the nature of sex-role stereotyping in children and the processes by which television portrayals could have a desired effect. In retrospect we find it useful to see our work as involving two broad steps: first, as it was influenced by a so-called consistency approach and second, when we shifted our emphasis to expectancy value theory and modeling.

## OUR BEGINNINGS WITH A
## CONSISTENCY THEORY BIAS

Most contemporary literature on sex-role stereotyping until the mid-1970s, as well as the best known intervention project (Guttentag & Bray, 1977), reflected a cognitive consistency orientation. As a consistency theory would suggest, individuals' behaviors are most probable when characteristics of self are consistent with the behavioral alternatives. Thus, a "masculine" boy would prefer football, working as a stockboy, and growing up to be in charge of things, whereas a "feminine" girl would prefer hopscotch, working as a babysitter, and growing up to be a housewife.

Much of the research until the time of "Freestyle" would lead one to believe that as young as nine, children were locking themselves into sex-role biases that would eventually deny them access to a great variety of adult occupations. Thus, a young girl might avoid math as "unfeminine" and lose forever the chance of someday becoming an engineer. Or the parents or teacher of this girl might discourage math training on the same grounds. Boys reared in the stereotype that only women do housework will be unprepared to negotiate the changing roles of men and women in the home. The effects of television have been readily integrated into this picture. For example, content-analysis studies of television show frequent examples of sex-roles stereotypes ("dumb" housewives being swayed to buy products, super "macho" men).[*] Children, being heavy viewers of television, experience massive doses of these stereotypes. Being impressionable and not seeing counterexamples, children internalize these stereotypes into their own beliefs and attitudes. They then behave in a way consistent with them.

Most of the attempts to gauge children's sex-role stereotypes also reflect a consistency approach in that the child's behavior is not directly addressed. In the case of personality characteristics, the child is asked instead to gauge concepts relative to various characteristics or traits, all previously selected by researchers because they reflect stereotypes found in the adult world. Bias in selecting mainly "male" or "female" characteristics defines stereotyping. Thus, in Guttentag and Bray's (1977) work a predominant "male" bias is associated with being strong, rough, a leader, and sloppy, to name a few characteristics, whereas a "female" bias incorporates such characteristics as obedient, good looking, weak, and a follower. In this particular scheme, there is an attempt to balance characteristics on the basis of social desirability. A child who rates himself or herself in a sex-role biased manner will presumably be biased in terms of activity interests, behavior toward others, and perhaps even occupational aspirations.

Some of our initial work in this area involved a replication of the use of the sex-role measures used by Guttentag and Bray. One reason was to see if the results they had obtained with children would have generality across the groups in our study, which included variations by ethnic group (Black, Anglo, Chicano) and age (mainly nine through 12 years). Of more theoretical interest to us, however, was what the results would tell us about the children's framework for judging sex-role characteristics. We felt that this would provide us with a first step in conceptualizing an intervention strategy, one mainly in consistency theory terms. We also sought to replicate parts of earlier work involving types of interests and activities (Holland, 1973; Rosenberg & Sutton-Smith, 1959, 1960) as well as occupations (Iglitzin, 1972; Schlossberg & Goodman, 1972). In loose terms, we were looking for "deep" mediators of stereotyping—that is, fundamental types of biases that would have generality across these domains. These would be the targets for our media intervention strategy.

The results of this phase of our project offered several relatively expected conclusions, but along with these were some serious challenges to our way of thinking, including the consistency approach. The highlights of these may be summarized as follows:

1. In simple cross-tabulation analyses, our results with the Guttentag and Bray scales were generally similar to their findings (also simple tabulations). There were a number of statistically significant boy-girl differences in the same directions reported by the previous researchers, indicating (within the limitations of this instrument) some evidence of stereotyping. Such stereotyping was greater—that is, more of a "male" or "female" bias—when children rated others as compared with self and most when rating the opposite sex. Useful for us was that these patterns generally obtained across ethnic and age groups.

2. Upon close inspection, a number of the personality rating differences, although statistically significant, could be argued as psychologically trivial in magnitude, especially if taken as a basis for predicting major biases in behavior. Differences were sometimes near the center of the scales, which added to the argument of their lack of importance in predicting behavioral differences. Further, scale reliabilities for ratings of self were low (by alpha, .45) as compared with ratings of others (.66 to .69) and especially as compared with activity interests (.80). The reliability problem also raised the issue, well stated by Constantinople (1973) and Bem (1974), that sex-role judgments are not basicially male versus female but along relatively independent dimensions.

3. A concept-by-scale factor analysis of the personality ratings revealed not only that concept (that is, self, most boys, most girls) and scales were interacting, but that the patterns were different for boys and girls. Thus, any data that are aggregated across scales for male-female comparisons are possibly not all that comparable, nor are aggregations compared across concepts.

4. Correlational comparisons across domains of personality ratings, activity interests, and occupational stereotypes, all obtained from the same children, did not reveal evidence that sex-role biases had substantial generality across these domains. There were modest relationships, yes, but evidence did not point toward deep sex-role mediators.

5. Although it was found that children would respond favorably to counterstereotypic sex-role characterizations in prototype television materials, the relations of sex-role stereotype measures

with these results did not particularly reflect what would follow from expectations based upon a consistency or balance theory approach.

Certainly, the above generalizations required considerable further evaluation. But in our interpretation, they led us to two important conclusions:

Sex-role stereotyping is probably a much more particularistic and superficial phenomenon in preadolescent children's beliefs, attitudes, and behaviors than a general and fundamental mediator.

Given the lack of evidence of a fundamental framework of sex-role biases found in the children's beliefs and attitudes, a cognitive consistency approach for conceptualizing such biases, as well as developing ways to modify them, would probably be unproductive.

Our extensive interview data also tended to support the above generalizations. In their conversations, children did not seem all that consistent in their sex-role biases when compared across concept domains. Although we felt that personality ratings were meaningful to most nine- through 12-year-olds, they interpret them quite particularistically (strong might be lifting a box), and they vary widely in these interpretations. (Try talking to them about leadership.) If this is indeed the case, then a television intervention strategy focused only upon broad personality abstractions (she is independent; they cooperate; he is a leader) is apt to be lost on the children. This coupled with the general problems of mapping one's way conceptually to behavior in a consistency model led us to concentrate next upon a model that directly addresses itself to behavior.

## EXPECTANCY VALUE THEORY AND MODELING

One of the more attractive features of Fishbein's expectancy value model is that it not only incorporates attention to behavior but still allows one to operate short of having to observe the behavior. This involves the concept of behavioral intention, the subjective estimate by an individual of the probability that he or she will be engaging in a behavior. Thus, for example, "I feel that it is probable that I will be mowing my lawn in the near future." Or a boy might estimate that he would be playing baseball, would not be sewing, or would be building a model. This does not ask whether they like to engage in the behavior; it is not an attitude. (Frankly, I hate mowing the lawn, but I will be doing it.) Another attractive feature of the behavioral intentions was that, if specific, they were most intelligible to children in our study.

Within expectancy value theory, behavioral intentions are taken to be predictable from a person's estimates of personal and social consequences of that behavior. Personal consequences are operationalized as simple good-bad attitudes, although there are strategies for studying their constituents. (That I dislike mowing my lawn is my attitude.) Social consequences are defined as one's estimates of how selected designated others will feel about the behavior, coupled with one's motivation to comply with these others. (My wife likes the lawn mowed and I am motivated to comply.) Both such dimensions were readily intelligible to the children in our age group. Given that children have a knowledge of the behavior, it is equally easy for them to register a "good" or "bad" or some gradation between these extremes. Of course, the social consequences require determining which others are important in the individual's life. But this is relatively easy with young children, for it is generally restricted to parents, siblings, other relatives, peers, and teachers.

Despite the attractiveness of this model, it did have two immediate shortcomings. Unlike consistency theory, there had been no tradition for applying it to sex-role stereotyping. Second, although expectancy value theory was developed in the context of persuasion studies, our interest in sex-role stereotyping would have to be integrated in such a way as to be related to the anticipated television intervention strategy. That is, if the model were used as a basis for conceptualizing how children learn from television, adaptations would have to be developed. Other than the procedural problems of facilitating children's use of the instruments, most of our research using expectancy value theory dealt with the above two issues. Highlights of the findings are summarized below.

1. Interpretable predictions (by multiple regression) can be obtained of children's intentions to engage in sex-typed behaviors using an expectancy value paradigm. Personal attitude is typically a statistically significant contributor, followed by parents as an additional predictor. Peers (defined as the best friend) are only an occasional predictor.

2. When behavioral intentions were separated into "male" (for example, mow lawns) and "female" categories (for example, babysit) and their prediction equations compared, results indicated that personal attitudes generally contributed more to predictions of girls' intentions than to boys'; that the stereotype influence presumably manifested in perceived social norms about "most boys" or "most girls" as significant others was not dominant as a predictor; and that differences in the individual equations, however, suggested that varying patterns of expected reinforcement for specific behaviors,

rather than some overall sex-stereotyped set of attitudes, were predictors of behavioral intentions.

3. When children were divided in terms of whether they expressed traditional (boys mow lawns) or nontraditional (girls mow lawns) sex-role beliefs about the behaviors, results again indicated a lack of major evidence of sex-role patterning in the predictor variables.

Although our applications of expectancy value theory were admittedly preliminary, the paradigm did allow us to predict behavioral intentions and to explore within a larger context than consistency theory the potential biases imposed by sex-role stereotyping. In general terms, our interim conclusion was that children's intentions to engage in various specific behaviors, many of them sex typed, are predictable from particularistic combinations of anticipated personal and social reinforcements, with little evidence of sex-role stereotyping being a fundamental contributor to those patterns.

Put another way, what we mean is that contrary to our assumptions in the consistency theory approach, we do not see sex-role stereotypes as a dominant force affecting the children's behavioral choices. Of course, such biases do affect personal attitudes and may be mixed in with estimates of, in particular, what "most boys" or "most girls" would sanction, all of which are researchable. But if stereotyping were a dominant force, we would have expected it to show up more visibly in the predictor patterns, particularly when data were separated by presumed sex-role biases in the activities or in children distinguished as traditional versus nontraditional. These conclusions presented a challenge to the development of materials designed to combat sex-role stereotyping. How could our findings with the expectancy value model be of use in plotting the media intervention strategy?

In line with the usual application of this theory in studies of persuasion and attitude change, we conceptualized a strategy that can be summarized as follows. First, select behavioral intentions that define particularistic counterstereotypical behaviors (girl: "I will go out for football"; boy: "I will take care of a baby"). Second, attempt to model those behaviors on television so that they will be identifiable and personally attractive to a child; that is, try to create a positive personal attitude toward them. Third, attempt to portray significant others in the presentation in ways that they can be identified as similar to the viewer's significant others and show clearly their positive (or negative) social sanction of the main model's performance of the intended behavior. And fourth, attempt to enhance the motivation to comply with that significant other. The third and fourth are in essence an attempt to influence the anticipated social reinforcement for the behavior.

The importance of modeling in our application of this paradigm served to underline our own experiences throughout the project in interviews with the children about whether they would like to emulate behaviors seen on the television screen. It also stressed the importance of recent research by others (for example, Reeves & Greenberg, 1977) into attributes of television characters that predict their modeling potential to child viewers. The overall generalization here was that characters who were like the children (age, sex, race)—perceived as physically attractive and strong and typical of most girls or boys—would be the best models. In pilot versions of "Freestyle," we had experimented with a recognizable adult male television star, expensive and highly entertaining animated figures, and even dancing trolls on an expensive musical set to convey the message of the problems of sex-role stereotyping. Yet none was as appealing to the children as a 13-year-old girl who was shown in a 30-minute drama ("Grease Monkey") trying to get and hold a summer job in a gas station. The surface appeal was the character as a potential model, coupled with a highly absorbing story. An effect of the program was not only the knowledge that a girl could work in a gas station but that it would be socially and personally rewarding to her. The children identified with the television character.

Our research into the role of modeling in the expectancy value paradigm was divided between replicating certain of the Reeves and Greenberg scales with our cast members and further researching children's responses to two of our final dramatic programs in which modeling and social reinforcement were jointly assessed. In general terms, we found:

1. Prior findings of the attributes that predict modeling were generally replicated with the use of a group of performers vying for roles in the present series. Some sex-role bias was revealed in that boys place more importance upon strength when rating boys and girls place importance upon being good looking.

2. The degree to which a child viewer related a significant other in a drama to his or her own respective significant other, and the degree to which this significant other was perceived as providing sanction for a behavior, predicted (modestly but reliably) a child viewer's intention to engage in that behavior.

Although our research into the modeling factors was preliminary at best, we felt that it provided the vital link for applying the expectancy value model to media experiences. We considered the result to be our first approximation to a model of at least one process by which television may affect a child's attitudes, beliefs, and behaviors. This model is graphically presented in Figure 14.1 and

FIGURE 14.1

Modeling from Television

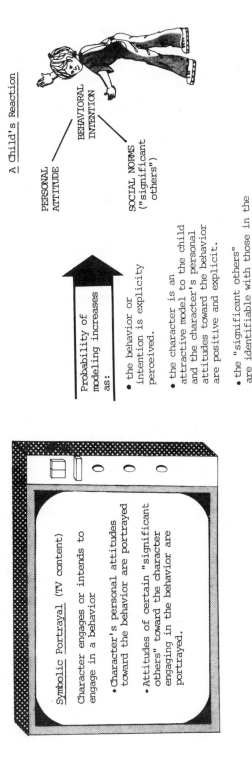

Symbolic Portrayal (TV content)

Character engages or intends to engage in a behavior

• Character's personal attitudes toward the behavior are portrayed

• Attitudes of certain "significant others" toward the character engaging in the behavior are portrayed.

Probability of modeling increases as:

• the behavior or intention is explicitly perceived.

• the character is an attractive model to the child and the character's personal attitudes toward the behavior are positive and explicit.

• the "significant others" are identifiable with those in the child's life, the motivation to comply with them is high, and their attitudes toward the behavior are positive and explicit.

A Child's Reaction

PERSONAL ATTITUDE

BEHAVIORAL INTENTION

SOCIAL NORMS ("significant others")

summarized as follows: The probability of children emulating behaviors experienced in television increases as a function of the modeling potential of a character (similar, strong, good looking, and so
on), anticipated personal reinforcement for the behavior, modeling
potentials of significant others, and perceived social reinforcement
from these significant others for the behavior.

Although we evolved to this way of thinking in the context of a
project to develop television materials, the above hypothesis could
apply equally well to what children may emulate in their everyday
experiences with television. If this hypothesis is supported, then
the quantities of males and females shown on television are considerably less important than the qualities portrayed. Behavior will be
most apt to be emulated from dramatic and realistic contents (not
variety shows, not cartoons) where a character has the attributes
for high modeling potential but, more important, where sufficient
content is presented to convey evidence of personal and social reinforcements for the behavior.

As for sex-role stereotyping, we still believe it to be present
in preadolescent children but not so fundamental as to serve itself
as a direct target for intervention strategies. Instead, we believe
that intervention will be best directed toward specific behaviors and
the child's anticipations of personal and social reinforcements.

# REFERENCES

Akamatsu, T., & Thelen, M. The acquisition and performance of a socially neutral response as a function of vicarious reward. Developmental Psychology, 1971, 5, 440-445.

Atkin, C. K., & Miller, M. M. Experimental effects of television advertising on children. Paper presented at the International Communication Association Convention, Chicago, April 1975.

Bakan, D. The duality of human existence. Chicago: Rand McNally, 1966.

Bandura, A. Influence of models' reinforcement contingencies on the acquisition of imitative responses. Journal of Personality and Social Psychology, 1965, 1, 589-595.

Bandura, A. Social learning theory of identificatory processes. In D. A. Goslin (Ed.), Handbook of socialization theory and research. Chicago: Rand McNally, 1969.

Bandura, A., Ross, D., & Ross, S. A. Vicarious reinforcement and imitative learning. Journal of Abnormal and Social Psychology, 1963, 67, 601-607.

Barkley, R. A., Ullman, D. G., Otto, L., & Brecht, J. M. The effects of sex typing and sex appropriateness of modeled behavior children's imitation. Child Development, 1977, 48, 721-725.

Barnett, R. C. Sex differences and age trends in occupational preference and occupational prestige. Journal of Counseling Psychology, 1975, 22, 35-38.

Bem, S. L. The measurement of psychological androgyny. Journal of Consulting and Clinical Psychology, 1974, 42, 155-162.

Bem, S. L. On the utility of alternative procedures for assessing psychological androgyny. Journal of Consulting and Clinical Psychology, 1977, 45, 196-205.

147

Bem, S. L. Theory and measurement of androgyny: A reply to the Pedhazur-Tetenbaum and Locksley-Colten critiques. Journal of Personality and Social Psychology, 1979, 37, 1047-1054.

Bem, S. L., & Lenney, E. Sex typing and the avoidance of cross-sex behavior. Journal of Personality and Social Psychology, 1976, 33, 48-54.

Bem, S. L., Martyna, W., & Watson, C. Sex typing and androgyny: Further explorations of the expressive domain. Journal of Personality and Social Psychology, 1976, 34, 1016-1023.

Berzins, J. I., Welling, M. A., & Wetter, R. E. The PRF ANDRO Scale user's manual. Unpublished manual, University of Kentucky, 1975.

Beuf, F. A. Doctor, lawyer, household drudge. Journal of Communication, 1974, 24, 110-118.

Bogardus, E. S. Measuring social distance. Journal of Applied Sociology, 1922, 9, 299-308.

Boynton, P. The vocational preferences of school children. Journal of Genetic Psychology, 1936, 49, 411-425.

Brim, O. G. Family structure and sex-role learning by children: A further analysis of Helen Koch's data. Sociometry, 1958, 21, 1-16.

Bronfenbrenner, V. Two worlds of childhood: U.S. and USSR. New York: Russell Sage, 1970.

Broverman, I. K., Broverman, D. M., Clarkson, F. E., Rosenkrantz, P. S., & Vogel, S. R. Sex-role stereotypes and clinical judgments of mental health. Journal of Clinical and Consulting Psychology, 1970, 34, 1-7.

Broverman, I. K., Vogel, S. R., Broverman, D. M., Clarkson, F. E., & Rosenkrantz, P. S. Sex-role stereotypes: A current appraisal. Journal of Social Issues, 1972, 28, 59-78.

Brown, D. G. Masculinity-femininity development in children. Journal of Consulting Psychology, 1957, 21, 197-202.

Bryan, J. W., & Luria, Z. Sex-role learning: A test of the selective attention hypothesis. Child Development, 1978, 49, 13-23.

Busby, L. J. Defining the sex-role standard in commercial network television programs. Journalism Quarterly, 1974, 51,
690-696.

Busby, L. J. Sex-role research on the mass media. Journal of
Communication, 1975, 25, 107-131.

Cantor, M. G. Women and public broadcasting. Journal of Communication, 1977, 27, 14-19.

Clark, C. C. Race identification and television violence. In G. A.
Comstock, E. A. Rubinstein, & J. P. Murray (Eds.), Television
and social behavior, Vol. 5, Further explorations. Washington,
D.C.: U.S. Government Printing Office, 1972.

Clark, E. T. Influence of sex and social class on occupational preference and perception. Personnel and Guidance Journal, 1967,
440-444.

Comstock, G., Chaffee, S., Katzman, N., McCombs, M., &
Roberts, D. Television and human behavior. New York:
Columbia University Press, 1978.

Constantinople, A. Masculinity-femininity: An exception to a
famous dictum. Psychological Bulletin, 1973, 80, 389-407.

Constantinople, A. Sex-role acquisition: In search of the elephant.
Sex-Roles, 1979, 5, 121-133.

Corporation for Public Broadcasting. Report of the task force on
women in public broadcasting. Washington, D.C.: Corporation
for Public Broadcasting, October 1975.

Costrich, N., Feinstein, J., Kidder, L., Marcek, J., & Pascale, L.
When stereotypes hurt: Three studies of penalties for sex-role
reversals. Journal of Experimental Social Psychology, 1975, 11,
520-530.

Courtney, A., & Whipple, W. Women in TV commercials. Journal
of Communication, 1974, 24, 110-118.

Cronbach, L. J. Coefficient alpha and the internal structure of
tests. Psychometrika, 1951, 16, 297-334.

DeFleur, M. L. Theories of mass communication. New York:
McKay, 1972.

DeLucia, L. A. The Toy Preference Test: A measure of series identification. Child Development, 1963, 34, 107-117.

Dohram, R. A gender profile of children's educational television. Journal of Communication, 1975, 25, 56-65.

Dominick, J. R., & Rauch, G. E. The image of women in network TV commercials. Journal of Broadcasting, 1972, 16, 259-265.

Douvan, E., & Adelson, J. The adolescent experience. New York: Wiley, 1966.

Fagot, B. I., & Littman, I. Stability of sex-role and play interests from preschool to elementary school. Journal of Psychology, 1975, 89, 285-292.

Fagot, B. I., & Patterson, G. R. An in vivo analysis of reinforcing contingencies for sex-role behaviors in the preschool child. Developmental Psychology, 1969, 1, 563-568.

Feshbach, N., Dillman, A. S., & Jordan, T. S. Portrait of a female on television: Some possible effects on children. In C. Kott (Ed.), Becoming female: Perspectives on development. New York: Plenum Press, 1979.

Fishbein, M., & Ajzen, I. Belief, attitude, intention, and behavior. Reading, Ma.: Addison-Wesley, 1975.

Flerx, V. C., Fidler, D. S., & Rogers, R. W. Sex-role stereotypes: Developmental aspects and early intervention. Child Development, 1976, 47, 998-1007.

Fling, S., & Manosevitz, M. Sex typing in nursery school children's play interests. Developmental Psychology, 1972, 7, 146-152.

Freuh, T., & McGhee, P. E. Traditional sex-role development and amount of time spent watching television. Developmental Psychology, 1975, 11, 109.

Frost, F., & Eastman, H. Project "Freestyle": National sites evaluation design. ERIC Document Reproduction Service. Los Angeles: The Annenberg School of Communications, 1978. 157-105.

Garrett, C. S., Ein, P. L., & Tremaine, L. The development of gender stereotyping of adult occupations in elementary school children. Child Development, 1977, 48, 507-512.

Gaudreau, P. Factor analysis of the Bem sex-role inventory. Journal of Consulting and Clinical Psychology, 1977, 45, 299-302.

Gerbner, G. Violence in television drama: Trends and symbolic functions. In G. A. Comstock, E. A. Rubinstein, & J. P. Murray (Eds.), Television and social behavior, Vol. 1, Media content and control. Washington, D.C.: U.S. Government Printing Office, 1972.

Gerbner, G. The dynamics of cultural resistance. In G. Tuchman, A. K. Daniels, & J. Benet (Eds.), Hearth and home: Images of women in the mass media. New York: Oxford University Press, 1978.

Gerbner, G., & Gross, L. Violence profile Number 6: Trends in network drama and viewer conceptions of social reality. Philadelphia: Annenberg School of Communications, December 1974.

Gerbner, G., & Gross, L. Living with television: The violence profile. Journal of Communication, 1976, 26, 173-194.

Gerbner, G., Gross, L., Jackson-Beeck, M., Jeffries-Fox, S., & Signorielli, N. Cultural indicators: Violence profile Number 9. Journal of Communication, 1978, 28, 176-207.

Gough, H. G. Identifying psychological femininity. Educational and Psychological Measurement, 1952, 12, 427-439.

Gough, H. G., & Heilbrun, A. B. Adjective Check List manual. Palo Alto, Calif.: Consulting Psychologists Press, 1965.

Greenberg, B. S. Children's reactions to TV Blacks. Journalism Quarterly, 1972, 49, 5-14.

Greenberg, B. S., & Dervin, B. Use of the mass media by the urban poor. New York: Praeger, 1970.

Greenberg, B. S., Heald, G., Wakshlag, J., & Reeves, B. TV character attributes, identification and children's modeling tendencies. Paper presented to the International Communication Association, Portland, Oregon, April 1976.

Gross, L., & Jeffries-Fox, S. What do you want to be when you grow up little girl? In G. Tuchman, A. K. Daniels, & J. Benet (Eds.), Hearth and home: Images of women in the mass media. New York: Oxford University Press, 1978.

Grusec, J. E., & Brinker, D. B. Reinforcement for imitation as a social learning determinant with implications for sex-role development. Journal of Personality and Social Psychology, 1972, 21, 149-158.

Guilford, J. P., & Guilford, R. B. Personality factors S, E, and M, and their measurement. Journal of Psychology, 1936, 2, 109-127.

Guttentag, M., & Bray, H. Undoing sex stereotypes. New York: McGraw-Hill, 1976.

Guttentag, M., & Bray, H. Undoing Sex Stereotypes: A how-to-do-it guide with tested non-sexist curricula and teaching methods. Unpublished manuscript, Harvard University, 1977.

Hathaway, S. R., & McKinley, J. C. Minnesota Multiphasic Personality Inventory: Manual. New York: Psychological Corporation, 1951.

Heatherington, E. M. A developmental study of sex of the dominant parent or sex-role preferences, identification and imitation in children. Journal of Personality and Social Psychology, 1965, 2, 188-194.

Heilbrun, A. B. Measurement of masculine and feminine sex role identities as independent dimensions. Journal of Consulting and Clinical Psychology, 1976, 44, 183-190.

Helmreich, R. L., Spence, J. T., & Wilhelm, J. A. A psychometric analysis of the personal attributes questionnaire. Sex-Roles, in press.

Helmreich, R. L., Stapp, J., & Ervin, C. The Texas Social Behavior Inventory (TSBI): An objective measure of self-esteem or social competence. JSAS Catalog of Selected Documents in Psychology, 1974, 4, 79.

Henderson, L., Greenberg, B. S., & Atkin, C. Sexual differences in giving orders, making plans and needing support on television. In B. S. Greenberg, Life on television, ed. by Melvin J. Voight. New Jersey: Ablex, 1980.

Holland, J. L. Making vocational choices: A theory of careers. Englewood Cliffs, N.J.: Prentice-Hall, 1973.

Holland, J. L.  A counselor's guide for the self-directed search.
Palo Alto, Calif.: Consulting Psychologists Press, 1974.

Iglitzin, L. B.  A child's eye view of sex-roles.  Today's Education,
December 1972, pp. 23-45.

Johnston, J., & Ettema, J.  Lessons from Freestyle: Creating
prosocial television for children.  Beverly Hills, Calif.: Sage,
in preparation.

Johnston, J., Ettema, J., & Davidson, T.  An evaluation of Freestyle: A television series to reduce sex-role stereotypes.  Ann
Arbor, Mich.: Institute for Social Research, 1980.

Kagan, J.  Acquisition and significance of sex-typing and sex-role
identity.  In M. Hoffman & L. Hoffman (Eds.), Review of child
development research (Vol. 1).  New York: Russell Sage, 1964.

Katz, E., & Lazarsfeld, P. F.  Personal influence.  Glencoe, Ill.:
Free Press, 1964.

Katz, P.  Correlates of sexual flexibility in children.  NIMH Final
Report, contract MH 29417, 1980.

Katz, P.  The development of female identity.  Sex-Roles, 1979, 5,
155-175.

Kelly, J. A., & Worell, J.  New formulations of sex-roles and
androgyny: A critical review.  Journal of Consulting and Clinical
Psychology, 1977, 45, 1101-1115.

Klapper, J. T.  The effects of mass communication.  New York:
Free Press, 1960.

Kobasigawa, A.  Inhibitory and disinhibitory effects of models on
sex-inappropriate behavior in children.  Psychologia, 1968, 11,
86-96.

Koblinsky, S. G., Cruse, D. F., & Sugawara, A. I.  Sex-role
stereotypes and children's memory for story content.  Child Development, 1978, 49, 452-458.

Kohlberg, L.  A cognitive developmental analysis of children's sex-
role concepts and attitudes.  In E. Maccoby (Ed.), The development of sex differences.  Stanford, Calif.: Stanford University
Press, 1966.

LaRose, R. J. Normative determinants of imitation. Unpublished doctoral dissertation, University of Southern California, 1979.

LaRose, R. Project "Freestyle": Baseline studies. Los Angeles: The Annenberg School of Communications, 1978. (ERIC Document Reproduction Service No. ED 157-107)

LaRose, R., Williams, F., Smith, K., Frost, F., & Eastman, H. Project Freestyle: Baseline studies technical report. (NIE Grant 400-76-0096). Los Angeles: University of Southern California, Annenberg School of Communication, 1978. (ERIC Document Reproduction Service No. ED 157-107)

Lazarsfeld, P., Berelson, B., & Gaudet, H. The people's choice. New York: Columbia University Press, 1948.

Leifer, A. D., & Lesser, G. S. The development of career awareness in young children. NIE Papers in Education and Work: Number One. Washington, D.C.: National Institute of Education, 1976.

Lemon, J. Dominant or dominated? Women in prime time television. In G. Tuchman, A. K. Daniels, & J. Benet (Eds.), Hearth and home: Images of women in the mass media. New York: Oxford University Press, 1978.

Levinson, R. M. From Olive Oyl to Sweet Polly Purebread: Sex-role stereotypes and televised cartoons. Journal of Popular Culture, 1973, 9, 561-572.

Liebert, R. M. Television and social learning. Some relationships between viewing violence and behaving aggressively. In J. P. Murray, E. A. Rubinstein, & G. A. Comstock (Eds.), Television and social behavior, Vol. 2, Television and social learning. Washington, D.C.: U.S. Government Printing Office, 1972.

Lippmann, W. Public opinion. New York: Harcourt-Brace, 1922.

Locksley, A., & Colten, M. E. Psychological androgyny: A case of mistaken identity? Journal of Personality and Social Psychology, 1979, 37, 1017-1031.

Long, M., & Simon, R. J. The roles and statuses of women and children on family TV programs. Journalism Quarterly, 1974, 50, 107-110.

Maccoby, E. E., & Jacklin, C. N. The psychology of sex differences. Stanford, Calif.: Stanford University Press, 1974.

Maccoby, E. E., & Wilson, W. C. Identification and observational learning from films. Journal of Abnormal and Social Psychology, 1957, 55, 76-87.

Maccoby, E. E., Wilson, W. C., & Burton, R. V. Differential movie-viewing behavior of male and female viewers. Journal of Personality, 1958, 26, 259-267.

Mackie, M. Arriving at "truth" by definition: The case of stereotype inaccuracy. Social Problems, 1973, 20, 431-447.

Maracek, J., Piliavin, J. A., Fitzsimmons, E., Krogh, E. C., Leader, E., & Trudell, B. Women as TV experts: The voice of authority. Journal of Communication, 1978, 28, 159-168.

McArthur, L. Z., & Eizen, S. V. Television and sex-role stereotyping. Journal of Applied Social Psychology, 1976, 6, 329-351.

McCandless, B. R. Children: Behavior and development. New York: Holt, Rinehart and Winston, 1967.

McNeil, J. C. Feminism, femininity and the TV series: A content analysis. Journal of Broadcasting, 1975, 19, 255-269.

Miller, M. M., & Reeves, B. Dramatic TV content and children's sex-role stereotyping. Journal of Broadcasting, 1976, 20, 35-50.

Mischel, W. Sex-typing and socialization. In P. H. Mussen (Ed.), Carmichael's manual of child psychology. New York: Wiley, 1970.

Montemayor, R. Children's performance in a game and their attraction to it as a function of sex-typed labels. Child Development, 1974, 45, 152-156.

Mussen, P. Early sex-role development. In D. Goslin (Ed.), Handbook of socialization theory and research. Chicago: Rand-McNally, 1969.

Nadelman, L. Sex identity in American children: Memory, knowledge, and preference tests. Developmental Psychology, 1974, 10, 413-417.

Nie, N. H., Hull, C. H., Jenkins, J. G., Steinbrenner, K., & Bent, D. H. Statistical package for the social sciences (2nd ed.). New York: McGraw-Hill, 1975.

Nolan, J. D., Galst, J. P., & White, M. A. Sex bias on children's television programs. Journal of Psychology, 1977, 96, 197-204.

O'Bryant, S. L., & Corder-Bolz, C. R. The effects of television on children's stereotyping of women's work roles. Journal of Vocational Behavior, 1978, 12, 233-244.

O'Donnell, W. J., & O'Donnell, K. J. Sex-role messages in television commercials. Journal of Communication, 1978, 28, 156-158.

Orlofsky, J. L., Aslin, A. L., & Ginsburg, S. D. Differential effectiveness of two classification procedures on the Bem Sex Role Inventory. Journal of Personality Assessment, 1977, 41, 414-416.

Parsons, T., & Bales, R. F. Family socialization and interaction process. Glencoe, Ill.: Free Press, 1955.

Pedhazur, E. J., & Tetenbaum, T. J. Bem Sex Role Inventory: A theoretical and methodological critique. Journal of Personality and Social Psychology, 1979, 37, 996-1016.

Perry, D. G., & Perry, L. C. Observational learning in children, effects of sex and model and subject's sex-role behavior. Journal of Personality and Social Psychology, 1975, 31, 1083-1088.

Pingree, S. The effects of nonsexist television commercials and perceptions of reality on children's attitudes about women. Paper presented at the annual meeting of the International Communication Association, Portland, Oregon, 1976.

Pingree, S. The effects of nonsexist television commercials and perceptions of reality on children's attitudes about women. Psychology of Women Quarterly, 1978, 2, 262-277.

Reeves, B., & Greenberg, B. S. Children's perceptions of television characters. Human Communication Research, 1977, 3, 113-127.

Reeves, B., & Lometti, G. E. The dimensional structure of children's perception of television characters: A replication. Paper presented to the International Communication Association, Chicago, 1978.

Reeves, B., & Miller, M. M. Distance in a multidimensional space as a measure of sex differences in children's identification with television characters. Paper presented to the International Communication Association, Portland, Oregon, April 1976.

Roberts, D. F. The nature of human communication effects. In W. Schramm & D. F. Roberts (Eds.), The process and effects of mass communication. Urbana: University of Illinois Press, 1971.

Rosecrans, M. Imitation in children as a function of perceived similarity to a social model and vicarious reinforcement. Journal of Personality and Social Psychology, 1967, 7, 307-315.

Rosenberg, B. G., & Sutton-Smith, B. The measurement of masculinity and femininity in children. Child Development, 1959, 30, 373-380.

Rosenberg, B. G., & Sutton-Smith, B. A revised conception of masculine-feminine differences in play activities. Journal of Genetic Psychology, 1960, 96, 165-170.

Rosenberg, B. G., & Sutton-Smith, B. The measurement of masculinity and'femininity in children: An extension and revalidation. Journal of Genetic Psychology, 1964, 104, 259-264.

Rosenberg, B. G., & Sutton-Smith, B. Family interaction effects on masculinity-femininity. Journal of Personality and Social Psychology, 1968, 8, 117-120.

Rosenkrantz, P., Vogel, S., Bee, H., Broverman, I., & Broverman, D. Sex-role stereotypes and self-concepts in college students. Journal of Consulting and Clinical Psychology, 1968, 32, 287-295.

Scheutz, S., & Sprafkin, J. N. Spot messages appearing within Saturday morning TV programs. In G. Tuchman, A. K. Daniels, & J. Benet (Eds.), Hearth and home: Images of women in the mass media. New York: Oxford University Press, 1978.

Schlossberg, N., & Goodman, J. A woman's place: Children's sex stereotyping of occupations. Vocational Guidance Quarterly, 1972, 20, 266-276.

Sears, R. R., Rau, L., & Alpert, R. Identification and child rearing. Stanford, Calif.: Stanford University Press, 1965.

Seggar, J. F., & Wheeler, P. World of work on TV: Ethnic and sex representation in TV drama. Journal of Broadcasting, 1973, 17, 202-209.

Sherif, M. The psychology of social norms. New York: Harper, 1966.

Sherif, C. W. , Sherif, M. , & Nebergall, R. E. Attitude and attitude changes: The social judgment-involved approach. Philadelphia, Pa.: Saunders, 1965.

Slaby, R. G. , & Frey, K. S. Development of gender constancy and selective attention for same-sex models. Child Development, 1975, 46, 849-856.

Smith, K. Project "Freestyle": Ad hoc: Fast-turn-around evaluation. Los Angeles: The Annenberg School of Communications, 1978. (ERIC Document Reproduction Service No. ED 157-106)

Snyder, M. , Tanke, B. D. , & Berscheid, E. Social perception and interpersonal behavior: On the self-fulfilling nature of social stereotypes. Journal of Personality and Social Psychology, 1977, 35, 656-666.

Spence, J. T. , & Helmreich, R. The Attitudes toward Women Scale: An objective instrument to measure attitudes toward the rights and roles of women in contemporary society. JSAS Catalog of Selected Documents in Psychology, 1972, 2, 66.

Spence, J. T. , & Helmreich, R. L. Masculinity and femininity: Their psychological dimensions, correlates and antecedents. Austin: University of Texas Press, 1978.

Spence, J. T. , & Helmreich, R. L. The many faces of androgyny: A reply to Locksley and Colten. Journal of Personality and Social Psychology, 1979, 37, 1032-1046. (a)

Spence, J. T. , & Helmreich, R. On assessing "Androgyny." Sex-Roles, 1979, 5, 721-738. (b)

Spence, J. T. , Helmreich, R. , & Stapp, J. The Personal Attributes Questionnaire: A measure of sex-role stereotypes and masculinity-femininity. JASA Catalog of Selected Documents in Psychology, 1974, 4, 127.

Spence, J. T. , Helmreich, R. , & Stapp, J. Ratings of self and peers on sex-role attributes and their relation to self-esteem and conceptions of masculinity and femininity. Journal of Personality and Social Psychology, 1975, 32, 29-39.

Sprafkin, J. N., & Liegert, R. M. Sex-typing and children's television preferences. In G. Tuchman, A. K. Daniels, & J. Benet (Eds.), Hearth and home: Images of women in the mass media. New York: Oxford University Press, 1978.

Stein, A. H., Pohly, S. R., & Mueller, E. The influence of masculine, feminine, and neutral tasks on children's achievement behavior, expectancies of success, and attainment values. Child Development, 1971, 42, 195-207.

Sternglanz, S. H., & Serbin, L. A. Sex-role stereotyping in children's television programs. Developmental Psychology, 1974, 10, 710-715.

Strahan, R. F. Remarks on Bem's measurement of psychological androgyny: Alternative methods and a supplementary analysis. Journal of Consulting and Clinical Psychology, 1975, 43, 568-571.

Streicher, H. W. The girls in the cartoons. Journal of Communication, 1974, 24, 125-129.

Tedesco, N. S. Patterns in prime time. Journal of Communication, 1974, 24, 119-124.

Terman, L. M., & Miles, C. C. Sex and personality studies in masculinity-femininity. New York: McGraw-Hill, 1936.

Triandis, H. C. Exploratory factor analyses of the behavioral component of social attitudes. Journal of Abnormal and Social Psychology, 1964, 69, 420-430.

Tuchman, G., Daniels, A. K., & Benet, J. (Eds.). Hearth and home: Images of women in the mass media. New York: Oxford University Press, 1978.

U.S. Civil Rights Commission. Window dressing on the set: Women and minorities in television. Washington, D.C.: U.S. Government Printing Office, 1977.

Vener, A. M., & Snyder, C. A. The preschool child's awareness and anticipation of adult sex roles. Sociometry, 1966, 29, 159-168.

Verna, M. E. The female image in children's TV commercials. Journal of Broadcasting, 1975, 19, 301-309.

Vidmar, N., & Rokeach, M. Archie Bunker's bigotry: A study in selective perception and exposure. Journal of Communication, 1974, 24, 36-47.

Wakefield, J. A., Sasek, J., Friedman, S. F., & Bowden, J. D. Androgyny and other measures of masculinity-femininity. Journal of Consulting and Clinical Psychology, 1976, 44, 766-770.

Walters, R. H., Leat, M., & Mezei, L. Inhibition and disinhibition of responses through empathetic learning. Canadian Journal of Psychology, 1963, 17, 235-242.

Walters, R. H., & Parke, R. D. Influence of response consequences to a social model on resistance of deviation. Journal of Experimental Child Psychology, 1964, 1, 269-280.

Walters, R. H., Parke, R. D., & Cane, V. A. Timing of punishment and the observation of consequences as determinants of responses inhibition. Journal of Experimental Child Psychology, 1965, 2, 10-30.

Ward, W. D. Process of sex-role development. Developmental Psychology, 1969, 1, 163-168.

Welch, R. L., Huston-Stein, A., Wright, J. C., & Plehal, R. Subtle sex-role cues in children's commercials. Journal of Communication, 1979, 29, 202-209.

Williams, J. E., Bennett, S. M., & Best, D. L. Awareness and expression of sex stereotypes in young children. Developmental Psychology, 1975, 11, 635-642.

Williams, F. Project "Freestyle": National sites results. Los Angeles: The Annenberg School of Communications, 1978. (ERIC Document Reproduction Service No. ED 157-104)

Williams, F. W. Sex-roles on TV: More than counting buttons and bows. Los Angeles: The Annenberg School of Communications, 1978. (ERIC Document Reproduction Service No. 172-106)

Wolf, T. M. Effects of live modeled sex-inappropriate play behavior in a naturalistic setting. Developmental Psychology, 1973, 9, 120-123.

Worell, J. Sex roles and psychological well-being: Perspectives on methodology. Journal of Consulting and Clinical Psychology, 1978, 46, 777-791.

Zanna, M. P., & Pack, S. J. On the self-fulfilling nature of apparent sex differences in behavior. Journal of Experimental Social Psychology, 1975, 11, 383-391.

# ABOUT THE AUTHORS

FREDERICK WILLIAMS is Professor of Communications in the Annenberg School of Communications at the University of Southern California where he was founding dean of the school from 1973 to 1980. Previously, he served on the faculties of the University of Wisconsin (1962-69) and the University of Texas (1969-73). He holds a doctorate in interdisciplinary communications studies from the University of Southern California (1962).

ROBERT LaROSE is now on the senior staff of Applied Communication Network, Inc., of Santa Monica, California. His doctorate was earned at the Annenberg School of Communications, University of Southern California, in communications theory and research in 1979, where he also served as a Research Associate. Prior to this period, Dr. LaRose was employed as a researcher by Arthur D. Little, Inc. He received his B.S. degree in engineering and psychology from Trinity College in 1972.

FREDERICA FROST is now a full-time consultant in evaluation and research on the staff of the East Whittier City School District, Whittier, California. From 1976 through 1979 she served on the research staff of the Annenberg School of Communications at the University of Southern California. She earned her doctorate in educational psychology at the University of Southern California in 1978. Prior to this period, Dr. Frost worked as a psychological researcher in programs involving mentally gifted minors.

# DATE DUE

| APR 15 '94 | MAR 7 '02 | | |
|---|---|---|---|
| APR 21 '94 | MAR 18 '02 | | |
| NOV 28 , 1 | | | |
| NOV 7 '94 | | | |
| DE DEC 14 '94 | | | |
| MAY 4 '95 | | | |
| APR 24 '95 | | | |
| NOV 13 '95 | | | |
| NOV 8 '95 | | | |
| MAR 19 '96 | | | |
| MAR 19 '96 | | | |
| APR 10 '97 | | | |
| APR 14 '97 | | | |
| MAR 31 '98 | | | |
| MAR 18 '98 | | | |
| MAY 9 '98 | | | |
| APR 30 '98 | | | |
| MAR 14 '02 | | | |
| | | | |
| GAYLORD | | | PRINTED IN U.S.A. |